DON'T BLAME THE
LETTUCE

DON'T BLAME THE
LETTUCE

Insights to help you
grow as a leader and nurture
your **workplace culture**

ERIC STUTZMAN
WENDY LOEWEN
RANDY GRIESER

ACHIEVE
PUBLISHING

Published by ACHIEVE Publishing
120 Sherbrook Street, Winnipeg, Manitoba R3C 2B4
www.achieve-publishing.com

Bulk discounts available. For details contact:
ACHIEVE Publishing at 877-270-9776 or info@achievecentre.com

This book is typeset in Minion Pro and Proxima Nova.
Printed with vegetable-based inks on 100% PCW paper.

ISBN: 978-1-988617-21-3
ISBN: 978-1-988617-22-0 (e-book)

Printed and bound in Canada
First edition, first printing

Book design by Ninth and May Design Co.

10 9 8 7 6 5 4 3 2 1

To our staff, who have taught us the most.

CONTENTS

INTRODUCTION

We believe that leadership development should be a priority for both aspiring and experienced leaders. Great leaders never stop learning – instead they seek opportunities for reflection, search for new ideas, and know they must keep growing in order to be effective in an ever-changing world. Effective leadership is important because it is an essential ingredient to creating healthy workplace cultures, which in turn sets the foundation for organizational success.

ACHIEVE Centre for Leadership (ACHIEVE), where we (the authors) are all leaders, is in the professional development training industry and offers training in the areas of leadership and workplace culture. We know that learning changes lives, and while we believe that attending online or in-person workshops is an impactful way to learn, another powerful way to develop and grow is through reading. This is due in part to the fact that reading is so accessible – you can read almost anywhere. Reading also makes it easy to access the knowledge of experienced thought leaders that might otherwise take you years to cultivate on your own. We have observed how our own thinking and practices related to issues of leadership are frequently propelled by what we read. In fact, we often exchange books with each other to enhance our leadership philosophies and management practices.

The insights found in this book have emerged from our own individual leadership journeys. They have come from many years of trial and error while leading our own organization, along with hours of focused, intentional reflection related to our leadership roles. Additionally, we have extensive experience coaching and training other leaders and consulting with organizations of various sizes to create healthy workplace cultures.

Our perspectives on leadership are undoubtedly shaped by our own leadership context, which is a midsized, non-unionized organization. We recognize that not all workplaces are the same – some organizations are large, while others are small; some are unionized, while others are not. So, you will need to think about how to apply our insights and suggestions to your own context.

We have honed our leadership practices and philosophies by working together and communicating about our own thoughts and struggles. In this way we have helped each other grow as leaders. And while each of the insights is written by us as individuals, you will see similarities in some of our approaches to leadership.

Some of the common themes you will find in these insights are people, relationships, and workplace culture. This is because we are driven by the belief that everyone should be able to like where they work. And to accomplish this goal, leadership qualities related to trust, empathy, listening, and communication are crucial. Yes, vision, strategy, and innovation are also important to organizational success – and we write about these things as well – but it's very difficult to be productive and thrive as an organization without first focusing on people.

Although *Don't Blame the Lettuce* was first a title of one of our insights, we also chose it for the book's title because its meaning is applicable to our philosophy of leadership. This phrase is inspired by the teaching of Thich Nhat Hanh. To paraphrase him, if a gardener plants lettuce and it doesn't flourish, the gardener can't blame the lettuce. Instead, they must look at their garden and determine what can be changed to ensure the lettuce has a healthy environment in which to thrive.[1] As leaders we must understand that our workplace is like a garden, and like all gardens it must be tended to so that our people can grow in healthy ways. And just like gardeners, we also need to develop our own knowledge, tools, and skills in order to help our workplaces flourish. Essentially, we must work to become master gardeners.

HOW THIS BOOK IS ORGANIZED

This book features insights on a variety of topics related to leadership. At the end of each insight, we have included questions for reflection, a practical application idea, and additional resources related to the topic. Whether you are reading this book on your own or with others, we encourage you to fully consider each insight and spend time reflecting on the questions and application ideas. To get the most from this book, we suggest developing a specific action plan for implementing the practical application ideas contained in each insight.

As part of the development of this book, we conducted a Leadership Development Survey, which over 1,100 leaders participated in. You will find results, insights, and quotes from those who participated in the survey incorporated into some of the insights under the Survey Quote and Survey Statistics headings. *A more detailed analysis of the survey can be found on page 262.*

While this book is helpful and applicable to the individual reader, our greater hope is that you will read it *together*, with others from your organization. Reading and learning with others is one of the best ways to integrate new approaches and ideas not just into your own practice as a leader, but throughout your organization. For example, implementing this type of collective approach may take the form of a weekly meeting to discuss each insight. Another option could be to take 10 minutes at the beginning of your regular meetings and have those in attendance share one key takeaway, question, or application from a previously assigned insight. In the same way that our own leadership development has been enhanced by talking about and working through the challenges and opportunities of leadership, our hope is that this book will be a resource that encourages collective leadership development within organizations as a whole – not just in individuals.

Our goal in writing this book is to inspire you to intentionally consider your approach to leadership, provide ideas to strengthen your leadership practices, and help you further develop your leadership philosophy. We also hope these insights will provide you with ideas for nurturing your workplace culture. While you may gravitate toward the insights that will help you cultivate the areas where you need the most support, our hope is that all of these insights will inspire you to action.

1
DON'T BLAME THE LETTUCE

BY ERIC STUTZMAN

I recently had an unsettling experience when I went to pick up some dry cleaning. The employee behind the counter couldn't find my garments, but instead of apologizing or saying she would look into solving the issue, she muttered under her breath, "I *hate* working here." Then she said things like, "I don't know what *they* were thinking," and when she couldn't find a pen, "Why don't *they* keep any pens around here?" After finding a pen, the conversation ended with me suggesting that she write down my name and number and have a manager call me the next day once my dry cleaning was in.

Curiously, I didn't feel angry as I walked away. Instead, I felt sad – sad for the missed opportunities for the person helping me and for the company she represented. Given her negative attitude toward her organization, it was obvious that the employee was unhappy. Something was clearly impacting her feelings about her workplace.

It would be easy to blame the employee for her poor customer service. Although she could have done things differently, I think finding fault with her would be an unhelpful place to start. Instead, it would be better to look at management practices and the organizational culture in which she worked. To paraphrase one of my favorite writers, Thich Nhat Hanh, if we plant lettuce and it fails to thrive, we do not blame the lettuce.[1] Instead, we look at the conditions in which it is growing and seek to change them so that it can thrive. If it needs more water, we give it water. If it needs different soil or sunlight, we might plant it in a different place. In the same way, we should not blame people when they make mistakes, act inappropriately, or, as in my situation above, provide poor customer service. Instead, we should seek to understand the conditions around them.

What I experienced at the dry cleaner was certainly a symptom of a deeper problem within the company. I wondered what opportunities had been missed to fully orient the employee to the work, support her capacity to problem solve, and show her how to resolve a missing clothing issue. It also struck me that there were likely missed opportunities to help her feel connected to her peers and respected for who she was. Her repeated use of "they" told me she did not feel she was part of the team.

People in organizations are like lettuce plants in a garden. Just as lettuce is influenced by conditions in the garden, so too are people affected by the conditions of their organization's culture. Our staff are not disconnected individuals, but rather interconnected parts of a whole organization. Their actions affect other people, and they are highly influenced by the culture around them. As leaders, we can make a real difference in the actions and experiences of our people by tending to the culture. Instead of blaming people when something goes wrong, we can change the conditions in our culture to elicit different behavior.

Throughout the years, I have frequently seen leaders blame their employees for a range of things. When something is broken on a job site, a leader might say, "It's broken because that crew doesn't care or take pride in their work." When someone comes in late, a leader might say, "That employee is lazy." When someone is involved in a conflict, a leader might say, "That employee is toxic."

While it is true that some employees may not show they care or act in lazy or combative ways, it's always more useful for the leader to look at the conditions that led to the employee's actions. When tools are broken at a job site and the leader diagnoses the issue as one of "care" or "pride," they should then ask themselves, *what conditions have I helped to create at the job site through my words or actions that make it difficult for people to care?* If an employee often comes in late, instead of judging them as lazy, it would be more fruitful to ask them if something else is going on in their life that might be leading to this behavior and then find ways to address those conditions. If an employee is engaging in gossip, the leader should be asking, what in the environment leads this employee to feel they need to act in this manner?

Let's also acknowledge that not all plants flourish in every garden – some are better suited for other climates or conditions. In the same way, not every person will be able to flourish in every type of organization. When we look first at our culture rather than blaming someone, we can see that we may not have the right conditions for them to grow. This leads to a different kind of conversation that is focused on fit rather than one that is founded on finding individual blame.

In order to have healthy workplace cultures where employees have the best chance to thrive, leaders must stop blaming and replace that impulse with curiosity and a need to understand. When examined through the lens of context, almost any behavior will be much more understandable. By seeking to understand the context behind a behavior, leaders can become much more proactive in addressing aspects of their culture that permit or lead to undesired behavior.

The work of a leader is really all about creating the conditions and setting the context in which staff can flourish. It is about preparing, nurturing, weeding, and feeding the soil so that the plants can thrive and do all the things we know beautiful, productive, healthy plants are

Just as lettuce is influenced by conditions in the garden, so too are people affected by the conditions of their organization's culture.

capable of doing. In order to have a healthy garden, we have to take responsibility for it; the same applies to our workplaces.

REFLECTION QUESTIONS

1. The last time someone disappointed you at work, did you focus more on the individual and their behavior or the workplace conditions that led to that behavior? What was the result of your focus?
2. If you were to think about your staff as plants in a garden, what could you and other leaders do to tend to the garden to create ideal growing conditions?

PRACTICAL APPLICATION

As you move through your week, notice when you are irritated with people or when you are tempted to find fault or blame. Write down your thoughts, and then write down a question or two that would help you look more deeply at the conditions in your culture that created space for that behavior. At the end of the week, make a list of things in your workplace culture that you could adjust or change to help your employees thrive, and then discuss them with your team.

ADDITIONAL RESOURCE

Peace Is Every Step: The Path of Mindfulness in Everyday Life by Thich Nhat Hahn (Bantam Books, 1992)

2

LESSONS ON INFLUENCE
FROM UNLIKELY PLACES

BY WENDY LOEWEN

Friday is date night for my husband and me. Typically, we order take-out, play a round or two of cards, and then watch a movie. The sign of a good movie is when I go to bed and can't stop thinking about it, which was the case for me this past weekend. My husband and I watched *The 33* (2015), a film based on the true events of the San José mine collapse in Chile.

The story is a testament to the power leaders have to inspire individuals and rally a team to work together. In the movie we see the astounding teamwork that occurred in 2010, when 33 miners were trapped 2,300 feet underground. The miners were stuck underground for 69 days, 17 of which they did not have contact with the outside world. Each miner had no one else besides the 32 others who were standing beside them in the dark, wet mine. As the story unfolds, we witness the profound influence of their leader, Luis Urzua, to inspire, mobilize, and motivate the group despite their difficult circumstances.

Three things in particular struck me about Urzua's leadership. First was the way he inspired his team by articulating his belief in a hopeful future. Second, he quickly organized the men into 12-hour shifts, rationing food and completing daily tasks. Third, he created opportunities for the team to share stories about their lives, play checkers, and participate in daily prayer sessions. Urzua's leadership through this crisis illustrates the three things I see as the crucial elements for positively capitalizing on the influence of any leadership position.

Provide Inspiration

Urzua was a reassuring influence on the group. He recognized that part of his role was to manage the fear of the miners and help them see beyond their current circumstances. He clearly communicated to the miners that their survival ultimately depended on helping each other. Urzua stressed that the group uphold each other's dignity and build each other up. He repeatedly reminded them to focus on the hope of a rescue and to remember their families and friends that were counting on them to come back home.

In our role as leaders, we need to encourage the people we supervise to persist despite the challenges they face and regularly remind them of our organization's mission, vision, and hope for the future. We should remember that we may not be aware of the obstacles that they are working to overcome as they complete their day-to-day tasks. We should be checking in regularly with staff to see what challenges they are facing and what struggles they are encountering. As we do so, we want to acknowledge their experience and remind them of the long-term goals and outcomes of their efforts. Hearing how their work contributes to our organization's mission serves as a long-term motivator despite the demands of the work.

Provide Structure

Under Urzua's leadership, the group divided work tasks, established living and waste areas, and even decided to use the lighting to create day and night conditions. For the first 17 days, they managed to stretch rations that were originally only intended to last for two days. This consisted of two spoonfuls of tuna, half a cookie, and half a glass of milk every two days. They drank water from a spring and a radiator. They broke into three teams, where they rotated in eight-hour shifts between sleeping, working, and playing – yes, playing!

In our workplaces we too need to have clear structure. Similar to the miners, when our staff face pressure or uncertainty, they look to their leaders to provide the stability that comes from structure. We can provide this by setting direction, outlining priorities, and articulating our clear expectations. Without these things it is easy for people to lose motivation and fall to chaos. Structure allows people to know what they can anticipate so they don't have to spend time worrying or wondering what to do; rather, they can focus on doing good work.

Provide Opportunities to Communicate

Urzua encouraged the miners to emotionally support each other by openly sharing their hopes and fears. The group of miners quickly began calling themselves "Los 33" and engaged in a daily ritual they referred to as "Show Your Cards" where they would voice their disagreements, highlight accomplishments, and make plans for what was next.

In all of our leadership roles, we too should be actively asking for the input, thoughts, ideas, perspectives, and opinions of the people on our team – those we agree with *and* those we don't. We should be doing this in our one-on-one check-ins as well as when we bring our team together. When we provide opportunities for people to gather, share their experiences, celebrate successes, discuss ideas, and wrestle with problems, we set the stage for effective teamwork to emerge.

On October 13, 2010, the last miner to be rescued from the collapsed mine was Luis Urzua. When he emerged, he said, "I have delivered you this shift of workers, as I agreed I would." He was greeted by the rescuers with a sign that read "Mission Accomplished." Urzua's leadership created the conditions that allowed for a celebratory ending. The leadership lessons from this story remind us of the power of leadership in valuing people and mobilizing them to work together. And when we do this, we can anticipate a team of motivated and inspired people who are energized to work toward the success of our organization.

REFLECTION QUESTIONS

1. Think of the experiences where you have learned valuable leadership lessons through books, movies, events, or other people. What were those lessons and how have they impacted your leadership?
2. In what ways do you inspire your team to persist when they face challenges? How are you providing structure for their work experience? And how are you creating opportunities for communication with the team(s) you lead? What more could you do?

PRACTICAL APPLICATION

This week, meet with your team and take 10 minutes to create a list of ways in which you could provide inspiration, give more structure, or communicate more effectively as a team. Commit to implementing at least three of your ideas in the following month.

ADDITIONAL RESOURCE

Deep Down Dark: The Untold Stories of 33 Men Buried in a Chilean Mine, and the Miracle That Set Them Free by Héctor Tobar (HarperCollins Publishers, 2014)

3
ENCOURAGING DISSENTING VOICES

BY RANDY GRIESER

Several years ago, I was doing a three-month check-in with a new employee. I had been working closely with him, and he had already shown great initiative and the ability to help us in a variety of new and unexpected ways. As a result, the feedback on his performance was glowing. He was therefore a little taken aback when I told him I had one issue.

He visibly braced himself for what he perceived would be negative feedback. However, what I said surprised him: "We need you to do a better job of telling us when you disagree with something. We need you to speak up and use your voice more when you have an idea or see something that's wrong." Upon hearing this, he noticeably relaxed as the feedback wasn't actually hard to hear. In fact, it was a positive and affirming message – it was as if I was saying to him, "You matter and your opinions matter."

One of the things I expect from our employees is for them to have a voice – and use it! When they see something that seems wrong or confusing, I want them to be confident and feel safe enough to say something about it. When they have a different way of looking at a problem or opportunity, I want them to share their thoughts, even if it's counter to my own thinking. I encourage them to use their voices because I've learned that the willingness of employees to disagree is crucial to our success as an organization. Without dissenting voices, we would make more mistakes and we wouldn't be nearly as innovative.

SURVEY QUOTE
A great leader is someone who talks to their employees and values the opinions of staff.

Most days I am moving fast – going from one task or project to the next and making multiple decisions on a variety of initiatives. Sometimes I forget something or am simply considering things from a different perspective. And sometimes I'm just wrong! These are times when I need to be able to rely on those around me and trust that they are willing to call me out and challenge my thinking and decisions.

In practice, these interactions are not conflictual but more matter-of-fact. They may sound like, "Hold on Randy, have you thought about …?" Sometimes hearing a new perspective ultimately changes my decision, and sometimes it does not. When it doesn't, I still value that the person cared enough to ask questions, raise a point for consideration, or directly challenge my thinking.

Some managers may think of dissenting voices as negative and irritating because they can be associated with being uncooperative and divisive. After all, most of us are taught from a young age to be polite, never interrupt people, and never question our elders. There may be some situations where a dissenting voice is not appropriate, but I don't believe this to be true for most situations.

Time and again I have seen how dissenting voices help our organization. Here are a few things I value about them:

- They help create opportunities for change and foster innovation
- They prevent mistakes and unintended consequences

- They bring forth new ideas
- They can turn good ideas into great ones

When someone is willing to disagree and share their honest opinion, it means they care about the work they are doing. As a leader you wouldn't let something go unsaid if you knew a mistake was impending or thought there was a better way to do something. When our staff are willing to raise their voices and offer opinions, it shows that they have passion and commitment to good work. This is a positive thing.

There are valuable and clear benefits for encouraging dissenting voices. No one would argue against fostering innovation and preventing mistakes, yet it is all too common for organizations to unintentionally (and sometimes intentionally) silence the voices of employees. Here are two signs your organization doesn't encourage dissenting voices:

People Walk On Eggshells

Is the general feeling in the workplace one of apprehension and worry? Are staff reluctant to give feedback, offer ideas, and share opinions because they are fearful?

I've learned that dissenting voices are silenced in a culture of fear. When employees are worried about making the slightest mistake or voicing disagreement for fear of punishment, dissenting voices will not flourish. To counter this, organizations need first to establish a culture that is void of fear – one that is built on a foundation of strong relationships and trust.

There Are Many "Yes" People

Do managers seek out opinions of those they know will affirm their way of thinking to the exclusion of others who are more likely to disagree? Some managers really dislike being challenged – after all, they are "the boss." For a variety of reasons, dissenting voices make these types of managers feel insecure. On the other hand, organizations that capitalize on dissenting voices have leaders who want their thinking to be challenged. These leaders have learned to embrace dissent, which results in their employees feeling confident enough to voice opinions and disagreements.

Organizations benefit on multiple levels when employees speak up and use their voices. In these workplaces, many bad decisions have been avoided because an employee wasn't afraid to say, "I think that's a bad idea," and new ideas were generated because they felt emboldened to say, "I've got an idea."

REFLECTION QUESTIONS

1. Are there times when people in your organization walk on eggshells around leaders? If so, why do you think this is the case?
2. When have you heard and seen the positive impact of dissenting voices at work? How could you be more intentional about encouraging dissenting voices in your organization?

PRACTICAL APPLICATION

Consider which employees are not using their voices and meet with them one-on-one this week to encourage them to speak up and share their opinions. Give them permission to disagree with you. Then make sure you thank them when they do speak up.

ADDITIONAL RESOURCES

In Defense of Troublemakers: The Power of Dissent in Life and Business by Charlan Nemeth (Basic Books, 2018)

TED Talk: "Dare to Disagree" by Margaret Heffernan

4
LEADER,
KNOW THYSELF

BY ERIC STUTZMAN

Often when we look back at our life experiences, we can see signs of our strengths emerging early on. I vividly remember getting into an intense conversation with a good friend one day in high school. He felt passionately about the issue and so did I, but our debate remained respectful. At the end of the conversation, he looked at me and said with admiration, "Eric, you should be a diplomat someday." While I no longer recall the content of our conversation, I remember wondering why he said that. Over the years since that time, I have learned that one of my greatest strengths lies in communicating about difficult things in a way that respects and makes space for others' perspectives and feelings. I have come to rely on that strength in my leadership journey, as well as on other strengths that I have discovered since then.

I have also discovered some things that I am not as good at. If a project requires someone to really focus and dive deep into a technical subject, it would be better to ask someone other than me to do that. When my leadership team is asked to come to a meeting with lists of ideas, mine is generally the shortest list. If you need someone to take command of a situation, there are others who are more comfortable doing this than me. It's not that I can't do these things, but rather that it's less natural for me.

Developing self-knowledge is a notion that is deeply entrenched in Western society. From the time of the ancient Greeks (and possibly before), philosophers have been extolling the virtues of "knowing thyself." However, developing self-knowledge is not an automatic process – it requires intentional effort and focus. But I believe the effort is worthwhile and that all leaders need to know their strengths and weaknesses for two reasons. First, through self-knowledge we learn how we can best contribute to our organizations – when I offer to do something in an area where I have strength, I will likely shine. Second, through self-knowledge we also learn what kinds of people we need on our teams to complement our strengths or make up for our weaknesses. For each of my areas of weakness, I can easily name people on my team I can rely on because they have strengths in those areas.

SURVEY QUOTE

First and foremost, a leader must be self-aware – aware of their values, beliefs, and, more importantly, their reasons for being in a leadership role.

One way to think about strengths and weaknesses is to consider where you have *aptitude* – an area of skill or a subject that you learn easily or that comes naturally for you. This could include being organized, gauging people's emotions, or even decorating your home. For me, one area I have a lot of aptitude in is communication. It is relatively easy for me to learn new ways of communicating, whether that is speaking in front of a group, chatting with a stranger, or having a difficult conversation. I also have aptitude in working with someone else's idea or plan and making it stronger. It's more natural for me to work with existing systems to improve them than to come up with a brand-new idea or process. *See You're Hired on page 59 to learn more about aptitude.*

On the flip side, you can recognize your weaknesses by thinking about skill sets or subjects that you find uninteresting or difficult. For instance, I have never been very interested in the mechanics of how things work. If my bike needs a tune-up, I take it to the bike shop. I could learn to do it, but I would find the process frustrating, not rewarding. When a technical issue comes up at the office, I am more than happy to let others deal with it who find that type of work interesting.

Knowing your weaknesses is as important as knowing your strengths. When you know where you are not strong, you can use that knowledge to build your team by asking for help and leaning on the strengths of others. This gives your team members a chance to shine and contribute using their strengths. Of course, for this to be possible, you also have to know the strengths and weaknesses of your team members. Through your own process of learning to know yourself, you can intentionally lead others to do the same by example, discussion, and invitation. At our office, we invite staff to reflect on their strengths at their annual goal-setting meetings with their supervisors. We also invite staff to learn and share about themselves in our annual team development session.

In my quest to know myself, I have found it helpful to rely on tools that others have developed for this purpose. There are many great options, but I have found two particularly helpful. The first is the CliftonStrengths Assessment. This tool looks at 34 areas of strength and ranks your personal strengths after you complete an online assessment. These strengths are in the four broad categories of Executing, Influencing, Relationship Building, and Strategic Thinking.

The other tool that I have found helpful is called the Enneagram. The Enneagram is a way of categorizing human personalities into types and then exploring their related strengths and weaknesses. It has been in development for hundreds of years, so there are a variety of books and online tools to explore this model. What I find helpful about it is the way it focuses on how you think and act when you are at your best, an average level of functioning, or your worst.

I have also found it helpful to listen to other people to find out about myself. Other people see me in ways that I do not see myself, especially those who I spend a lot of time with. They see what I do well, and they see where I struggle. To listen, we need to put away our pride. My spouse would tell you that I get things done quickly in the kitchen, but that I sometimes lack sufficient care and attention to detail that would make the result a little better. I know that I am also like that at work sometimes. I work quickly and get a lot done, but I miss some of the important details. This is hard for me to admit, but I know it is true. And that knowledge means that I need to humble myself, ask for forgiveness from time to time, and enlist the help of others who see the details and know how to slow down.

The journey to self-knowledge is not an effortless one, but it is worthwhile. It is not easy because it requires us to be truthful to ourselves and to others. It means not undervaluing or overvaluing our strengths while at the same time not minimizing our weaknesses. We should focus on becoming the best we can be, given our unique set of aptitudes. The journey to self-knowledge is worthwhile because it helps us become clear about who we are and more confident in how we can best lead within our organization.

REFLECTION QUESTIONS

1. How much time have you spent learning about your strengths and weaknesses? In what ways have you learned about them? Is there more you could do?
2. In what ways do you or could you rely on others from your team to help you with your areas of weakness? How could you connect with other team members about drawing on each other's strengths?

PRACTICAL APPLICATION

Spend some time thinking about your strengths and weaknesses by going somewhere quiet and making a list of things you know you do well. As you make your list, consider subjects that you learn easily and things in life that interest you the most. This list will help you discover areas of aptitude. Then make a list of things that you're not interested in or that frustrate you. As you consider this second list, look for themes or areas of aptitude that are not as strong for you – these may be related to your weakness. Finally, consider how you can offer your team more of what you are good at and invite others to contribute from their areas of strength.

ADDITIONAL RESOURCES

StrengthsFinder 2.0 by Tom Rath (Gallup Press, 2007)[*]

The Honest Enneagram: Know Your Type, Own Your Challenges, Embrace Your Growth by Sarajane Case (Andrews McMeel Publishing, 2020))

---

[*] An added benefit is that when you buy a new electronic or hard copy of this book, you will also receive access to the StrengthsFinder online assessment tool.

5
R-E-S-P-E-C-T

BY WENDY LOEWEN

When my three children were young, there was no shortage of arguments around who would get the first cookie or who got to choose which game we would play. I sometimes wondered how they would relate to each other as adults. Would they be kind? Would they appreciate each other's perspectives? Would they listen to each other? Would they be respectful?

As they were growing up, my husband and I tried to model respect as we knew that we were their primary influencers. We didn't always get it right, but it was a high priority and we strived to do better each time we missed the mark. My children are now adults and have matured into thoughtful, caring, and respectful people. I believe that leaders, like parents, don't have to be perfect, but we do have the responsibility to set expectations and model how respect will be lived out in our workplaces. However, this is no easy task.

In building a respectful workplace, it can be easy for leaders to resort to speaking in platitudes like "Everyone matters on our team," "We work to maintain an environment of respect," or "We aspire to be respectful in all our interactions." Although these statements are not inherently bad, they don't give us any tangible markers for *how* to be respectful. That is why it is far more important that we become

When we lead by example, we set the stage to become the change we want to see and that others will follow.

practical about what respect is by naming what the target behaviors are and then demonstrating and living out respect in both our actions and words.

A quote by Mahatma Gandhi on my office wall reminds me of how I understand my role as a leader: "You must be the change you want to see in the world." I believe that when we lead by example, we set the stage to become the change we want to see and that others will follow.

There will be times when we must call on policy and procedures when employees have behaved disrespectfully and when we have to move to discipline. However, in my experience, many workplaces rely on these reactive measures too quickly, often without exploring the most proactive stance – to provide the example of respect ourselves.

Following are four ways to build a respectful workplace by being the change you want to see in your organization.

Be Patient

As leaders, it is helpful to remind ourselves that everyone makes mistakes. At the same time, we want to take seriously the responsibility of keeping the relationships between people in our organization respectful. This means we should gently hold people accountable for comments or behaviors that are disrespectful, and then allow the person to do the work necessary to make changes.

Early in my career, I remember being in a meeting where a new staff member said something in jest that was inappropriate. Later when I spoke privately with her and asked about the negative comment, she was sincerely apologetic and thankful it had been brought to her attention. She committed to changing her behavior and asked that I remind her should she slip up again. In the weeks to come, we had several conversations about how to speak to others respectfully. She was open to these conversations and received each one as a learning opportunity.

Our ability to be patient means that we should anticipate that there may be growing pains as we build a respectful work environment. Rather than seeing the mistakes people make along the way and the resulting need for a difficult conversation as indicators that we have fallen short, we should see them as opportunities to make a positive change. As leaders, we want to model and practice patience as we support our staff to build a workplace where everyone feels safe and cared for.

Celebrate Differences

Respect encompasses more than just tolerance of or putting up with certain individuals or behaviors – it is rooted in the belief that human beings are innately valuable. It means showing consideration of others by leaning into and even exploring the differences we encounter. When we respect our staff, we safeguard their dignity and appreciate their differences, even when we don't fully understand them. Respect requires us to welcome differences and recognize that they contribute to a vibrant workplace. We should be curious, ask questions, and get to know those we lead – not just learn what they do but also understand *who they are.*

In our organization, one way we celebrate differences is through sharing about our diverse backgrounds. We have begun to hold informal monthly lunches where one staff member volunteers to share about their culture or background, or significant parts of their identity. Each sharing session is followed with an opportunity for the rest of the group to ask questions or show their appreciation for what they have learned. Recent sessions included one person sharing about their Indigenous heritage, and at another, a staff member shared their experience of social and medical transitioning to align with their gender identity. This has been a rich experience for all of us as we seek to learn more about each other, and these sessions have increased our awareness of the diversity on our team. When we intentionally learn about each other and express interest and gratitude for each other, we go a long way toward cultivating a respectful workplace.

Remember That Intent Is Not the Measuring Stick of Respect

If our intent was not malicious but the effect was negative, we are still responsible for acknowledging, apologizing for, and changing our behavior – even if we meant no harm. This is true for our staff, and it is equally true for leaders. No one is perfect, and if we have not said sorry or checked in on the impact of our actions lately, we probably aren't setting the example we want.

Recently, I sent what I thought was a succinct email to a staff member. Later in the day they approached me to ask if I was upset with them. I was taken back as I had intended to be clear and transparent in my communication. I quickly thanked them for coming to me, apologized for the impact of my hastily sent email, and promised to be more mindful in the future. It is our role as leaders to be aware of the impact of our words and behaviors and to be responsive to those around us – no matter how well-meaning our intentions may be. It is the impact of our actions that matters, not only our intent.

Broaden Your Community

Respect is an active process of engaging people of different backgrounds, with the goal of increasing our awareness. We naturally size people up quickly because of their stature, ethnicity, gender expression, fashion choices, accent, and more, and then we put them into boxes because of these characteristics. As leaders, we should be vigilant and broaden our experiences with people and organizations with varied backgrounds. The more we build relationships with diverse groups of people and listen to new ideas, the more accepting we will be in our workplaces and communities. Being accepting and building relationships benefits those who have historically experienced exclusion and enriches our organization as we gain input from a variety of perspectives by making it safe for everyone to contribute.

In our own experience at ACHIEVE, we have found that it is especially important to listen deeply to and understand the stories of invisibility, pain, and oppression experienced by people who belong to minority groups. This includes people who are racialized and marginalized due to their race, gender, sexuality, ethnicity, age, or disabilities. Through listening we build connection and show others that we value who they are and what they have to say. One of the ways our organization has worked to broaden our community is through supporting the work of non-profit organizations that are striving to address societal injustices. We make donations, sponsor events, and partner with them to provide training. We recently hosted a conference, for example, and donated the proceeds to a non-profit agency that works to reduce poverty by helping Indigenous and immigrant women start their own businesses.

A respectful workplace contributes to employee well-being and makes our world a better place in which to live and work. When employees feel respected, they can focus their energy on the important role they play in making our organization a success, rather than their energy being consumed by responding to disrespectful behavior. As leaders, we play a pivotal role in modeling what this kind of respectful workplace will look like. We start by embodying the change we want to see, being mindful of our impact, and welcoming, seeking out, and engaging openly with the full range of human expression. When we do this, we set the stage to work together with our staff to build a respectful workplace.

REFLECTION QUESTIONS

1. Reflect on a recent unhealthy workplace situation or incident that may have been experienced as disrespectful. How did leadership respond and what was the result?
2. How could you lead by example and be the change you want to see when it comes to creating a respectful workplace?

PRACTICAL APPLICATION

Meet with your team or direct reports individually and share with them your commitment to creating a culture of respect in your workplace. Let them know you would appreciate it if they would speak with you when you say or do something that does not land well for them. When they do, listen and thank them for their feedback.

ADDITIONAL RESOURCES

Inclusion: Diversity, The New Workplace & The Will to Change by Jennifer Brown (Purpose Driven Publishing, 2016)

TED Talk: "Are You Consciously Creating a Culture of Respect?" by Shalini Sinha

6

THE VALUE OF VALUES

BY RANDY GRIESER

Consider this scenario I've seen played out multiple times. Someone from leadership, human resources, or the board of directors has decided it's time to create or update the organization's value statements. To get leaders excited about defining the organization's values, a date is set for meeting off-site at some high-end retreat center – golfing and spa fees are included. Only senior-level leaders are invited, and while they enjoy the amenities of the center, they also spend time developing and even getting excited about their new values. However, when they return to the office and proudly announce the organization's new set of values, they are confused as to why employees aren't excited and don't buy into them. Eventually the new values fade away – even for those involved in creating them.

While this scenario likely isn't your organization's exact experience for how your value statements were developed, in too many workplaces, staff and sometimes even leaders don't view values as helpful or important. This is unfortunate since having well-developed values that are communicated and applied regularly can be a great resource for organizations. This is because values clarify how the organization and its staff should behave. They provide the framework for making decisions and for how staff should interact with customers, clients, and

Values can't feel like something imposed by management or a board because then people are less likely to own them.

each other. But without buy-in, values aren't helpful.

I have learned that when you want buy-in from staff on major issues, it is far better to involve *everyone* in the discussion. At ACHIEVE, our original values were developed collectively with staff and leaders about a decade ago. They quickly became our guide for how things are done and how we interact with each other. We use them to guide our hiring practices, performance management, and, occasionally, the process of letting staff go. They are not just words on a wall – leaders *and* staff know them and appreciate them. And while new employees weren't a part of our value-development process, they are oriented to the history of each value so that the expectation to live them out is clear.

A few years ago, we realized that while many of the values we originally articulated still fit for us, it was time to check in and revisit them. And even if they did all still fit, having a conversation about them would serve to clarify and cement their importance to our organization. This is why we set an intentional time for *everyone* to revisit our values together.

There were two critical things that we did to set the tone for this meeting. First, the discussion of values was the only reason for the meeting – it wasn't just an agenda item tacked on to the end of a long list of other things. Because it is rare for us to have an all-staff meeting that is focused only on one item, everyone viewed it as important and prepared accordingly. We instructed staff to spend time considering our values ahead of time and whether our existing values still fit or if there were new ones that we should add. At the meeting, it was clear that people had taken this instruction to heart.

The second thing we did was ensure that *everyone* – ranging from the CEO to our newest employee of two months – was involved in the discussion and would have a part in clarifying and agreeing to our values. It was important that employees weren't just watching from the sidelines. This was because we knew that for organizational values to be effective, everyone needed to agree to and be on board with them. Values can't feel like something imposed by management or a board because then people are less likely to own them.

In larger organizations, it can be difficult to involve everyone in a values discussion, and it is likely impossible to do it in the same way we did. However, there are still creative ways to involve employees in the process. At minimum, staff should have the opportunity to voice their opinions in a survey format, and any groups that meet to discuss values should include diverse representatives from all areas of the organization.

At our values meeting, we discussed and sometimes debated about whether our existing values were still true and meaningful. After a lengthy and meaningful conversation, we removed one of our values that no longer seemed to fit and added a new value: *flexible*. We realized that we had developed a culture that expects everyone to jump in and help when needed. We reject the not-in-my-job-description mentality. We are willing to help each other out on any task because we know it will help us with our mission. This had become so important to us that we wanted to see it reflected in our values.

Currently, these are our five values:

Embody	We practice what we teach
Engaged	We care about our mission and each other
Flexible	We pitch in where needed
Productive	We get things done individually and collaboratively
Receptive	We are open to feedback and improvement

These five values are fundamental to our identity. They guide our decisions and interactions, and we hold each other accountable to them. A key memory of that values meeting for me was how the day resulted in a feeling that we are all part of something special, and that we are all moving in the same direction. Having clearly defined values helps solidify and align how we work on both our daily tasks and our long-term vision.

REFLECTION QUESTIONS

1. What are your organizational values and how were they developed? What has been the impact of either involving or not involving employees in this process?
2. How do your organizational values help guide your organization? What more could be done to make sure they are relevant and meaningful to everyone?

PRACTICAL APPLICATION

Have a meeting where the discussion of values is the *only* item on the agenda. Consider if your workplace's values fit for the current reality of your organization. If they fit, consider how you are using them to guide decisions and interactions. If they no longer fit, plan to bring people together to update your values.

ADDITIONAL RESOURCES

"Communicate Your Purpose & Values" in *The Culture Question: How to Create a Workplace Where People Like to Work* by Randy Grieser, Eric Stutzman, Wendy Loewen, and Michael Labun (ACHIEVE Publishing, 2019)

The Advantage: Why Organizational Health Trumps Everything Else In Business by Patrick Lencioni (Jossey-Bass, 2012)

7
NAVIGATING
ROUGH WATERS

BY ERIC STUTZMAN

A few years ago I faced an intense windstorm with seven of my friends on a canoe trip. At the end of the 10-day trip, we encountered a problem at our final lake crossing – the waves in the middle of the lake looked far too big for our canoes. Before heading out, we stopped to talk about our options. After much discussion about alternative routes, we made the difficult decision to set up camp on a small island near the shore and wait out the wind.

Around mid-afternoon the following day, the wind suddenly died down and we hurriedly packed our gear into our canoes and set out, keeping another island in view along our route in case we needed to take shelter again. Halfway across the lake, the wind suddenly intensified and struck us broadside from a different direction. In minutes we found ourselves in four-foot swells.

After a few minutes of exhausting paddling, we realized we could not keep paddling toward the far shore. So we implemented our alternate plan, turned our canoes, and rode with the wind toward the backup island. After sheltering for another few hours, the wind finally died down near sunset, and we finished the short paddle to our destination on the far shore, where we celebrated arriving safely.

As leaders we are often faced with external storms that force change upon our organizations. Whether they come from changes in government policy, massive shifts in technology such as the rise of artificial intelligence, or the effects of something like a natural disaster, we must be ready to face the challenge.

When we are confronted with intense pressures to change, we have three options available to us as we move into the future: we can either fight the change, drift with it, or steer a new course. Each of these options prompts a different set of questions, which leads to different sets of actions and results. When leaders are forced to respond to these significant external pressures, they will make choices, often unconsciously, about which of these paths to follow. I believe we should make conscious choices that move us in the direction of the third option.

Option 1: Fight Change

Like canoeists trying to push ahead against intense winds and threatening waves, some people will resist the changes in their work world in the vain hope of returning to an idealized yesterday or sticking to their plans. This will look like organizations trying to do their work and provide services in exactly the same way they did before they were confronted with the pressures of change.

Organizations that fight change will likely be asking themselves questions that ultimately contribute to a lack of progress and staff feeling stuck, such as:

- "How can we reinforce our current processes?"
- "Who is responsible for how things have gone?"
- "How can we meet the same targets we set prior to the change?"

Instead of consulting with staff, leaders will ask them to keep working as though nothing has changed and dismiss the efforts and credibility of those who try to change. This will create resistance and unhappiness when people realize that their workplaces have not kept up with changes in expectations about how to behave and meet their clients' needs. They will fear for their jobs and the organization's survival.

Large organizations, or those with long-held traditions or rigid bureaucracies, may be particularly drawn to this approach. After all, it is natural for leaders to resist change that causes pain within the organization, and it is difficult to change the trajectory of a large organization. However, getting stuck in this approach will severely limit an organization's ability to succeed in the long run.

SURVEY STATISTICS

According to our survey respondents, leaders from small organizations adapt to change more quickly than those from large organizations. What follows are the percentages of respondents who agree with the statement, "When the world outside of my organization changes, our leaders are quick to adapt," by organization size:

- **72%** from organizations with 1–15 employees
- **65%** from organizations with 16–150 employees
- **56%** from organizations with 151+ employees

Option 2: Drift with Change

Many organizations will find themselves adrift in the storms of change, like canoeists simply trying to survive without a clear plan about how to get to their destination. They will conform to the changes in societal expectations but may be slow to adapt. Their actions will be reactive to the new circumstances and many opportunities will be lost.

Organizations that drift with change will be asking themselves questions that may help them stay afloat but will probably not lead them down new and productive paths:

- "What can we do to simply survive?"
- "What *must* we change in order to continue doing the work we have always done?"

- "What changes do we have to make so we can keep doing what we were doing before?"

Staff will be asked to think about how they can adapt the way they do their work. The focus of their work will be on fixing and tweaking existing products, work protocols, and services. Leaders will be focused on helping staff adapt to present realities. They will feel nervous and worried about whether their workplaces will survive, but also hopeful that they can get back to doing what they do best.

I believe that many organizations choose this option by default as they scurry to stay afloat. In fact, most organizations will start here as they struggle not to capsize in the early days of being confronted with intense pressure to change. However, those who want to thrive will quickly move away from this approach and into the third option.

Option 3: Steer a New Course

The third and most hopeful and productive option for organizations is to take control of their destiny and steer a new course for themselves, creating different plans – much like my friends and I did when we faced the windstorm. These organizations will quickly realize that their mission and values, their organizational steering system, can be harnessed to make plans, chart a new course, and thrive.

These organizations will be asking themselves a totally different set of questions that will lead them to be both responsive to the current conditions and help them imagine new ways forward. These questions will sound like:

The collective experience, wisdom, and creativity of staff is an incredible asset that all leaders should tap into when faced with pressure to change.

- "Given how our customers' or clients' expectations have changed, what can we offer right now?"
- "What opportunities do we see for our organization and how are we going to work toward them?"
- "What strengths do we have from which we can build our future?"
- "What is the next best move available to us that is consistent with our core values?"

Using questions like these, leaders can ask staff to creatively imagine and shape the future of their organization with them. They can work with staff to step out of their patterned comfort zones to adapt to the new situation. These organizations can change their patterns of work while staying rooted in their strengths, their mission, and their vision for a better future. Staff may still experience the stress and worries of the changes – especially at first – but they will also be committed to their work and optimistic for their organization's future.

I believe that this final option requires visionary and courageous leadership. Any organization can choose this approach to navigate change pressures. However, they must realize that their services and products will likely need to change, be willing to let go of practices that no longer serve them, and ask this different set of questions *with* their staff.

I have learned that to successfully guide an organization through significant change, leaders need to realize that they cannot and should not try to do it alone. The collective experience, wisdom, and creativity of staff is an incredible asset that all leaders should tap into when faced with pressure to change. In our own experience at ACHIEVE, when working through pressures like financial stress, disruptions to how we deliver services due to technology advances, or the COVID-19 pandemic, our staff often come up with ideas that leaders would have missed on their own. Together we work to figure out ways to change and innovate amid the constraints brought on by these storms. And not surprisingly, because we now have a history of *steering a new course* through changes, this framework has become the norm when we face new pressures to change.

REFLECTION QUESTIONS

1. What strategies or tools have you used in the past with your staff/colleagues to support the change process? How did it work? What would you improve?
2. What skill-building, reflective conversations, or capacity building might assist your team now in becoming better prepared to effectively steer a course when faced with significant change pressures?

PRACTICAL APPLICATION

As you go about your work this week, think about the ways your organization is being pressured to change. Then write out the questions in Option 3 above and use them to focus your thoughts, and ask your team what their thoughts are as you problem solve and move forward.

ADDITIONAL RESOURCE

Leading Change: An Action Plan from the World's Foremost Expert on Business Leadership by John Kotter (Harvard Business Review Press, 2012)

8

WHY VULNERABILITY
MAKES A BETTER LEADER

BY WENDY LOEWEN

Early in my leadership role at ACHIEVE, I had an experience that shaped my understanding of what it means to be a good leader. A new staff person made a mistake that cost our organization a few hundred dollars. Understandably, she was embarrassed and anxious about it. When she told my colleague (her boss) what had happened, my colleague's response surprised me. He said, "Thank you so much for telling me. I'll probably make a mistake by lunch time today. Just last week, I sent out a contract with the wrong price on it that cost us nearly a thousand dollars in lost revenue. It's not a good feeling and I don't want to do it again, so I've worked on improving my process so it doesn't happen again. I know you'll do the same. Thanks again for telling me."

SURVEY QUOTE

A great leader is able to admit when they don't know the answer or when they have screwed up.

I suspect this short conversation was as memorable and impactful for our new employee as it was for me. It highlighted the importance and power of vulnerability. I had always looked to my colleague as an example for what kind of leader I wanted to be, and although I already deeply respected him, this admission cemented my trust. It reiterated that he was someone I could speak openly with about my own mistakes and trust with my own struggles at work.

Seeing my colleague acknowledge his mistake also had a significant impact on my own understanding of leadership. For many years I had the idea that a leader was a kind of superhero – one that knew it all, was close to perfect, had endless reserves of energy, and did not make mistakes. Sadly, many of us have been trained to believe that the best leaders need a larger-than-life persona and an air of perfection. And we have come to believe that we should reveal only the good parts of ourselves, to always be poised and polished, and to look like we have it all together.

Vulnerability is often avoided by leaders, especially if we buy in to the belief that it is a sign of weakness. However, this is not what being vulnerable as a leader entails. Brené Brown, a researcher who has spent the past two decades studying vulnerability, describes it as "uncertainty, risk, and emotional exposure."[1] These elements are all present in leadership. In a leadership role, we are sometimes unsure how our message or direction will be received, we take calculated risks where the outcomes are not guaranteed to be successful, and our emotional responses are always being watched. Most leaders know that uncertainty, risk, and emotional exposure are part of what we signed up for. However, some leaders cover up these elements by being cool and aloof and putting on an air of superiority. As a result, they are perceived as inauthentic – which is the exact opposite of vulnerability.

People are always looking for cues to see if they can relate and connect with those around them. No one connects with someone who stands on a pedestal, doesn't have any weaknesses, and never admits to making a mistake. Consciously or unconsciously, we are always deciding if a person warrants our trust by asking internal questions like: *Are they who they appear to be? Are they authentic? Are they honest?* How we answer these questions helps us decide how vulnerable we will be with them and how much is safe to reveal.

When we sense that someone is honest, authentic, and caring, we open ourselves up and come to trust them. Conversely, when we perceive someone as being inauthentic, we close off, retreat, and make sure we keep ourselves safe.

Many leaders I speak with feel disconnected, even with their own leadership team. We have often heard that it's lonely at the top. I believe a lack of vulnerability contributes to the feeling of isolation leaders often experience as they try to maintain an image of infallibility and perfection. They keep their struggles to themselves, feel poorly about mistakes, and expend energy trying to play the part of the competent leader. Ultimately this leads to a lack of connection and sense of loneliness.

This same principle of vulnerability leading to connection and trust holds true for the relationship between leaders and staff as well. Staff are watching and waiting for us to show that we are human, just like them. As leaders, it is our responsibility to model vulnerability. When we do, we build trust, which in turn creates the safety needed for our staff to be vulnerable themselves.

When leaders are vulnerable with staff and openly speak about mistakes, they create an atmosphere where honest conversations can take place and we can learn from and fix mistakes quickly. In building an environment where open conversations happen, we also need to prepare ourselves for the fact that some of these conversations will be uncomfortable.

When we do hear unsettling information from staff, such as something they are struggling with or a mistake they made, we should recognize that they are being vulnerable and demonstrating their trust in us. How we respond will determine whether they continue to be open and honest with us, or whether they close off.

Vulnerability allows us to have honest and even difficult conversations that deepen our human connection. By embracing vulnerability, leaders and those we supervise are liberated from the need to exert unnecessary energy trying to maintain an unrealistic image. Instead, we can invest our efforts into building strong relationships and learning from our mistakes, which allows us to do good work together – and this is what ultimately fuels organizational performance.

REFLECTION QUESTIONS

1. What does vulnerability mean to you? In what ways have you demonstrated vulnerability? What was the impact on you and on others?
2. Going forward, are there ways that you can be more purposeful in supporting staff to be vulnerable? What would that look like?

PRACTICAL APPLICATION

Watch Brené Brown's TED Talk, "The Power of Vulnerability," with your staff. Then discuss the level of vulnerability you show and experience with your leadership team. Share your commitment to creating a workplace where people are encouraged to be vulnerable and be sure to model vulnerability yourself. Ask for support when you need it, give voice to your struggles, and if you make a mistake, be transparent and ensure that you do not try to cover it up.

ADDITIONAL RESOURCES

Daring Greatly: How the Courage to Be Vulnerable Transforms the Way We Live, Love, Parent, and Lead by Brené Brown (Gotham Books, 2012)

TED Talk: "The Power of Vulnerability" by Brené Brown

9

LET IT GO

BY RANDY GRIESER

One of my favorite memories as a leader was when a young employee I was increasingly relying on for more important and challenging tasks told me, "You know, Randy, I'm not qualified to be doing half the tasks you're giving me." I could tell by her tone and body language that, while she enjoyed the challenges I was providing, she also wanted to ensure that I knew I was trusting her with important tasks that she hadn't been formally trained to do. My response to her was that I trusted her and believed in her abilities, and that she shouldn't worry so much about her perceived lack of "qualifications" because I didn't. Throughout her time with us, she excelled and proved herself capable of tackling every task I gave her.

I have always seen helping others to develop as one of my most important responsibilities as a leader. And I have learned that one of the best ways to foster development is by delegating meaningful and important tasks. Delegating these sorts of tasks says, "I trust you" and "I value you." In my experience, when I show that I trust and value others, they rise to the challenge of the task. However, that does not mean that I delegate without thought – particularly when I am unfamiliar with a person and the task is crucial to our function as an organization.

I have been the most senior leader within our organization and have overseen our marketing efforts since our inception. In conversations with others, I've learned that marketing is not an area most leaders delve into or hold up as important enough to merit much of their attention. As such, marketing is often delegated to less senior staff. I, however, have always enjoyed my role in our marketing efforts and firmly believe that branding and marketing are critical for organizational success, so I had not delegated leadership in this area to other people. But after close to 15 years of leading these efforts, I decided it was time for me to let go.

While I had already delegated some of my other tasks to people over the years, they were only those I hadn't been as passionate about – and some I even disliked. In other words, letting go was easy. Usually, the person I was delegating the task to was excited about the opportunity and ended up doing an equal or much better job with it than I had. However, letting marketing go was different for me. For one, I really like doing it; and two, I'm really good at it. As a result, delegating, although it has been a slow process, was a new and sometimes difficult experience for me.

This may beg the question of *why* I wanted to let this go. After all, if I like it and am good at it, what's wrong with continuing to do it? In my first book, *The Ordinary Leader*, I make the point that "A leader's greatest area of strength risks becoming an organization's greatest weakness when they refuse to let go at the right time. All tasks need to be candidates for possible delegation. Just because we like to do something, and we're good at it, doesn't mean we should continue doing it."[1]

Overseeing our marketing efforts takes a lot of time, and it would have gotten in the way of other high-value tasks had I continued doing it. In collaboration with the rest of our leadership team, we determined that, right now, the greatest benefit I can give our organization is to spend more time focused on writing and speaking. And to do these two areas well, I needed to let go of marketing.

Through this process I've learned a few things that may be helpful as you consider letting go of tasks that you are both good at and enjoy, and even those you don't:

Assess the Level of Interest

Staff will usually be excited when they are selected for a task – they should feel empowered by you asking them. If they are not interested or only express lukewarm interest, it may be an indicator of a larger issue related to workload, aptitude, or what brings them satisfaction. Before delegating, make sure they are committed and on board with the task.

Educate

When training the person you are delegating the task to, be sure they know not just *what* you are doing but *why* you are doing it in the way you are. Share the key insights you've learned and the history of why certain decisions were made regarding how the task functions.

Go Slowly

Instead of handing over everything all at once, take small steps – make sure the person you are delegating to becomes fully comfortable with one area of the overall task before adding another. This is particularly important for larger and more complicated tasks.

Be Open-Minded

Recognize that the person you are delegating the task to may have some new ideas that are good and should be implemented. It's natural for people looking at something for the first time to have fresh ideas you haven't even considered – this is a positive thing. When new ideas are implemented and if they work, celebrate that success.

Express Confidence

Let the person know that you believe in them and their ability to do the task. People typically live up to – or down to – the expectations we place upon them. One of the most powerful ways to build confidence is to express your positive expectations.

Be Okay with Some Mistakes

Recognize that someone likely won't initially do a new task as perfectly or quickly as you, and that mistakes may happen. When they do, affirm the person's efforts, correct their mistakes, and express confidence in their abilities.

Letting go of something you like to do and are good at is rarely easy, but when done right, it can be a win-win for everyone. It frees up time for you to focus on what's most important in your role as a leader, and it helps those you are delegating to develop their skills and empower themselves to grow and evolve.

REFLECTION QUESTIONS

1. What areas of your work have you delegated to others? Have you delegated things you enjoy? What has been the result for you and the person you delegated to?
2. What does your organization most need you to do with your time? Are you spending enough time doing it? If not, consider what else you could delegate to free up more time to focus on that important task.

PRACTICAL APPLICATION

This week, delegate something meaningful. First, consider the various talents of the people you lead against the difficult tasks that are currently on your plate. Then, consider the possible tasks you could give to these people. And finally, go through the six points identified above. Remember, the goal here is not only to free up more of your time – it's also to develop the skills of others.

ADDITIONAL RESOURCES

"Delegation" in *The Ordinary Leader: 10 Key Insights for Building and Leading a Thriving Organization* by Randy Grieser (ACHIEVE Publishing, 2017)

Deep and Deliberate Delegation: A New Art for Unleashing Talent and Winning Back Time by Dave Stitt (21CPL Productions, 2018)

10
LEARNING FROM OTHERS

BY ERIC STUTZMAN

When my grandfather, Amos, died at the age of 95, we gathered as a family to mourn and celebrate his life. In the week after his death, we spent many hours with my grandmother, sifting through his possessions and reflecting on his life. One of the things we found was a bag full of masonry tools behind the driver's seat of his little red pickup. Amos worked as a masonry contractor for 50 years in a small city in Oregon and retired at the age of 75 – he specialized in building fireplaces. He identified with his craft for his entire life.

Seeing the tool bag full of trowels, gloves, and measuring tools reminded me that a decade earlier I had the opportunity to work on a brick project with my grandfather. He was already into his mid-80s, and I wanted to learn about his craft. My parents agreed to have us build a brick column around a light post in front of their house. Looking back, I see important leadership lessons in the week that I spent with him building that column.

From the outset, there were many lessons to learn. When I asked where to start, my grandfather replied that the first thing we needed was a clear idea of the finished project in our heads. He said we needed to consult with my parents about how the column should look so that they would be happy with the result. "After all," he reminded me, "whatever we build out of brick is going to be there for a very long time." So, we sat down to discuss and envision the project with my parents.

Once the vision was fixed in our minds, we were able to move into the planning phase. We drew the column, took measurements, made calculations, and cleared working space for the project. Then we went shopping, gathered the necessary materials, and set up our tools in the driveway.

"What's next?" I asked.

"Well," he said, "we need to make sure that we start level. A small error at the foundation will get worse as we build up." He impressed upon me how important it was to start the project correctly in order to get a good result. We measured some more and ensured that our foundation was level.

Next, he showed me how to mix mortar. "This is important," my grandfather said. "We have to add a cap full of dish detergent to make the mortar easier to work with. This keeps it from hardening too fast." Had I been reading directions for mixing mortar in a book, I suspect I wouldn't have found this piece of advice. But as a master of his craft, my grandfather had learned ways to make the job easier that he could now pass on to me.

"Now," he said with a smile, "we can begin to lay the bricks." And with a sure and steady hand, my grandfather dipped his trowel into the mortar, laid some of it down, and set a brick. After demonstrating this process a few times, he handed me the trowel and said, "You try." It looked easy, so I was shocked to find out how difficult it actually was. What took him seconds took me minutes. He patiently corrected my movements and gave me space to continue. Every now and then he would demonstrate again. Then he would return to his lawn chair in the shade nearby and watch my progress.

Layer after layer, the brick column began to rise. After each layer, my grandfather would ask, "Is it level? Is it square? Is it plumb?* We

---

* "Plumb" refers to whether the structure is vertically straight or true to a vertical plane.

have to make sure we are building it true. Each layer must be correct or the layers that follow will be thrown off." His questions helped me to reflect on what I was doing and to see and correct my mistakes. He never criticized me – he just asked questions and showed me what to do when I needed help.

Throughout the project, my grandfather continued to teach me. "In masonry," he explained, "finishing occurs throughout the project. As you lay each layer of brick, you have to use a pointing tool to make the mortar look good." I learned that you have to think about what it will look like at the end right from the beginning of the project. You can't be sloppy and go back to clean it up later – mortar doesn't work that way. And so we finished our column layer by layer as we worked. When our project was done, the pillar looked great from the bottom to the top.

As I've thought more about leadership over the last several years, this memory has served as a helpful reminder of the leader I'd like to be. My grandfather was not trying to teach me to be a better leader, but his method of teaching illustrated the kind of supportive guidance I wanted to instill in my own work.

He began by focusing on creating a clear vision through consulting interested people. This made the resulting work easier to do, and we ended up with something that our customer (my parents) valued. As a leader, I need to have a clear vision and remember to consult those who will be impacted by a project. Through consultation, we serve our staff and our clients or customers more effectively.

My grandfather also emphasized always working with the end in mind and finishing as you go – our work was never sloppy, and we didn't have to spend time fixing things later. When we finished, we were truly *done*. When I apply this approach to my work as a leader, it means attending to the details of a project along the way, insisting that we do things correctly at each step, and always thinking about how the end result should look.

Perhaps the most valuable thing I learned came from the way he guided me through the work. First, he demonstrated. Then he let me try. He corrected my imperfect attempts without any blame or frustration – he just showed me again and let me make another attempt. His patience was amazing. I see this approach as replicable in most or, perhaps, *all* workplaces. People will follow if their leaders demonstrate, if they are given space to try, and if they are shown how to correct their work in a way that doesn't involve blame.

SURVEY QUOTE

The best leaders are those who say, "Come on, let's go on this journey together," rather than "Come on, follow me, let's go."

Throughout the building process, Amos asked questions that helped me assess what I was doing and see what he was seeing. The questions allowed me to think critically about my work and respond without defensiveness. They helped me *self-correct*. My grandfather didn't have to demand and criticize – he simply had to help me understand what he was seeing. To me, this was exemplary leadership. All leaders should be asking questions that help people see and understand their work objectively and with clarity so that they can self-correct and grow.

Years later, that brick column I built with my grandfather still stands in front of my parents' house. It's beautiful. And it reminds me that leadership doesn't need to be complicated. Leadership happens when we *create clear vision*, when we *show the way* and let people try, and when we *ask questions that help people see* their work with clarity and understanding.

REFLECTION QUESTIONS

1. Consider leaders or mentors who have shown you how to do something. How did they show you? What was effective or ineffective about their approach? What can you learn from them?
2. Going forward, how can you enhance your mentoring/teaching skills with your staff as part of your own leadership development?

PRACTICAL APPLICATION

As you work with your team members this week, consider how you can show them what type of work you are asking for. Then remind yourself to get out of the way so your staff can try out what you've shown them. Ask questions that help people see their work clearly and self-correct. Notice what happens as you focus on showing them the way.

ADDITIONAL RESOURCE

Decoding Greatness: How the Best in the World Reverse Engineer Success by Ron Friedman (Simon & Schuster, 2021)

11

FIND THE HIDDEN
SOURCES OF CONFLICT

BY WENDY LOEWEN

In my consulting work, I regularly help organizations with issues of conflict. In a recent workplace mediation, I saw firsthand how easy it is to misdiagnose the source of conflict. The situation was explained to me as an interpersonal dispute between two employees. One had criticized the other for an error in their work, and the conversation quickly became heated. Over the next few weeks, there were other instances of mistakes and hostility between the two. Their manager noticed the tension and stepped in. After a quick assessment, he reprimanded the employee for what he also assumed was sloppy work and set clear expectations. The employee agreed to be more careful. The manager, however, was not sure how to resolve the tension between the two employees and I was asked to mediate.

In my early discussions with both parties, it became clear that the mistakes were linked to something more than sloppiness. I encouraged the manager to speak with the employee who made the mistakes with the intent to understand the situation and consider how he could be a support to that person. With this new approach, he quickly found out that health issues were impacting the employee's ability to focus. The errors were important to address, as was restoring the relationship between the two employees in conflict, but only focusing on the presenting problem would not deal with its source. The manager had misdiagnosed the situation. He responded to what he saw (the poor work), acted on this limited view, but left the root (a health issue) untouched.

This story exemplifies why leaders should be aware that interpersonal conflict might have roots in other places. As we seek to manage conflict in our workplaces, we need to make sure we identify the true causes. If we don't, we run the risk of dealing with the presenting problem while leaving one or more of the sources of the conflict untouched. Conflict has many layers, and being aware of what these are can help us figure out what is really going on and see more clearly what our next steps might be. Here are some areas to consider as you search for potentially hidden sources of conflict:

Sources of Conflict

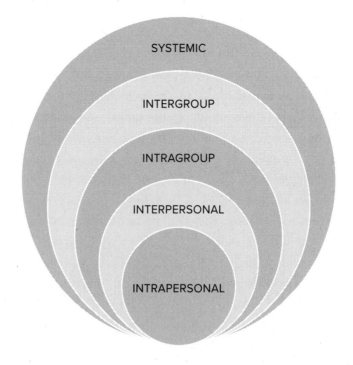

Intrapersonal

Intrapersonal conflict is internal conflict that may be caused by issues like financial worries, family stressors, tragedy, or health issues that put strain on a person. Because of these stressors, people may be predisposed to conflict in other situations or with other people. Unless our staff choose to tell us about their struggles, we may neglect this as a contributing factor to conflict in our workplaces.

A supervisor recently told me that one of their staff was found in the bathroom crying on a regular basis. Her colleagues were annoyed with her for being "oversensitive." The supervisor initiated a conversation and found out that the individual was struggling with mental health issues, and together they were able to decide on a helpful course of action.

Interpersonal

Interpersonal conflict is the result of unhealthy interaction patterns between two people. It typically happens because of disagreements, misunderstandings, or personality differences. For example, two people may find themselves in conflict because they disagree on how to allocate a departmental budget. Other times people find themselves in conflict because they misinterpret each other's words or actions.

For example, one staff asks the other when they will be done with their part of the project. From that question, their coworker infers that they don't trust them to get their work done on time. In reality, their coworker's intent is to make sure the project is on track. This kind of misunderstanding can be the start of interpersonal conflict. Or sometimes staff are in conflict because of personality differences in how they express themselves, levels of interaction they prefer, or even how they like to structure their work.

Intragroup

Intragroup conflict takes place between two or more members within an existing group. Typically, we see intragroup conflict emerge on

Conflict in our workplace alerts us that something is not working.

working teams or within organizational departments. Intragroup conflict often erupts in response to different ideas of how a task should be completed or how procedures should be conducted, as well as differing goals or competing priorities.

A recent team I worked with was tasked with creating a new strategy for a project. However, their manager did not provide clear guidance and the members in the group began arguing about how to proceed. One person on the team was sure that his course of action was the best while several other team members disagreed, and the conflict continued because they could not reach an agreement. The leader had failed to offer ongoing support and did not check in on how the group was doing. As a result, he was unaware of what was occurring. And when the team fell behind on the project, he reprimanded them for their tardiness but neglected to address the growing intragroup conflict that began due to his unclear directions.

Intergroup

Intergroup conflict is where a person's identity in one group puts them in conflict with another group. In workplaces this often manifests as what we refer to as "silos." This can happen when various groups do not understand how each group fits into the bigger picture of the organization, appreciate the other's contribution, or know who is responsible for what. This often results in unhealthy relationships or competition between the groups.

Several years ago, I worked with a school where the teachers and custodians were annoyed with each other. Both sides were bothered by the other for many reasons, but one big reason was the lack of attention to recycling. Each side was annoyed because the other did not take care of the recycling in their classrooms until it was overflowing. The problem was that the task was never clearly assigned to either group. But the issue had gone beyond just recycling bins and developed into a them-against-us mentality. When a new teacher started, they were told that *those custodians* were lazy; and, when a new custodian started, they were told that *those teachers* were whiners. Essentially, the identity of being a teacher or custodian automatically put the new employee in conflict with the other group. Without clarifying roles and expectations or highlighting their joint contribution to the school, the intergroup conflict escalated.

Systemic

Systemic conflict is a result of injustices such as biased laws, a lack of relevant policies, or prejudices both in our workplaces and larger society. It is easy to identify systemic biases when you look for "isms" – rac*ism*, age*ism*, sex*ism* – these are all examples of systemic conflict. This type of conflict also tends to create and perpetuate conflict in all the previously outlined sources.

Several years ago, I worked with a manufacturing company where racism was rampant. One employee told me that it was common for him to hear derogatory comments about the smell of his ethnic food. In one instance, he said this led to a fist fight in the lunchroom. The owner of the company was frustrated with what he deemed to be unruly employees. I was asked to mediate a conversation between the two individuals. After several conversations, it became apparent that the source of the conflict was much larger than the two people – it was systemic. In order to address the issue, the company needed to examine the racism in their workplace culture.

Conflict in our workplace alerts us that something is not working. As leaders we need to pay attention when we see conflict emerge and address issues as quickly as possible. And in order to respond in a helpful manner, it is imperative that we not let the appearance of conflict hide what other factors might be contributing to the situation.

We do this best by pausing, reflecting, asking lots of good questions, and listening to what we hear. Remember that what presents as one thing might actually be the result of something else. This knowledge can help us understand and address the true causes of conflict as we strive to create and maintain a healthy workplace.

REFLECTION QUESTIONS

1. Think of a recent conflict you have experienced at work. In retrospect, can you think of some of the sources of conflict that may not have been so readily apparent?
2. What are the typical issues that cause conflict in your workplace? What might this indicate about the sources of conflict in your workplace that you should be paying attention to?

PRACTICAL APPLICATION

The next time you become aware of a conflict in the workplace, consider each of the sources of conflict and how they may be contributing to the situation. Sit down with the parties involved to discuss the roots of the conflict. Be prepared to ask questions and to listen as you clarify your understanding of the situation. Then spend some time mapping out a plan that addresses the sources of the conflict.

ADDITIONAL RESOURCE

The Dynamics of Conflict: A Guide to Engagement and Intervention by Bernard Mayer (Jossey-Bass, 2012)

12

ADVANCING YOUR VISION BY SAYING NO

BY RANDY GRIESER

My son recently left home for college, and as part of the transition to this next phase in his life we sorted and organized a lot of his belongings. While we were packing up some of his keepsakes, we stumbled upon his baby book and read it together. In it was a collection of firsts – his first steps, his first friend, and his first words. We chuckled when we were reminded that his very first word was "no." In fact, it was one of his most frequently used words throughout his early childhood. It doesn't take a child psychologist to recognize that this was his first word because he regularly heard it from his parents.

While I don't say no as frequently as I once did to my now adult son, I do find that, as a leader, it's important for me to say no from time to time. Granted, I do give more context with my staff as opposed to the single word "no" I used with my child. When I say "no" now, it is either preceded by discussions or followed by explanations. While there are various reasons I say no to things, I have learned that often when I say no, it's because the request or idea being asked about won't help us achieve our vision.

I regularly hear a version of the following story from a variety of industry leaders: Someone in the organization has an idea for a new product or service and at first glance it's not a bad idea, but on closer inspection, it doesn't really support the vision of the organization. Nonetheless, people are excited about putting energy in to implementing it, and so the leader says, "Let's go for it" and puts their stamp of approval on the project. Days, weeks, and maybe months go by. Energy that used to go to other areas has now been transferred to this initiative and those other areas begin to suffer as a result – and the fallout is sometimes significant. If the new project isn't yet implemented or isn't working out, people usually start to wonder why they decided to do this new initiative. The leader begins to realize that by shifting the organization's attention to something new and exciting, focus has been taken away from their core initiatives that best help them work toward their vision.

The message here is not that the leader should have simply said no to the initial idea – it's that they should have asked, "How does this new idea help us achieve our vision?" *Vision* should drive the focus of our work and be at the core of any decision to implement a new idea. Whether a leader says yes to a new initiative or not should first be tested against the question of, "If we do this, will it help us achieve our vision?" And if it doesn't, the leader needs to say no.

SURVEY QUOTE

The best leaders have a clear vision for how to move forward into the future and are able to clearly communicate the goals for how to achieve that vision.

At ACHIEVE we are in the business of professional development training. But when you take a closer look, our organization's focus is actually quite narrow. *We envision a world where everyone likes where they work,* so all our training materials, books, and resources are created to work toward this vision. This means that we are focused on topics such as leadership, workplace culture, and conflict resolution because each of these subjects contributes to building workplaces where people like to work.

So, when someone has an idea for a new workshop about physical fitness or personal finance, no matter how excited they are and regardless of whether we could market and sell the course, the answer is pretty simple – it's no. We don't and won't provide physical fitness or personal finance training because those types of initiatives don't support our vision. And by adding unrelated themes to our core topic areas, we would hinder our ability to make our vision a reality.

To effectively use your vision in this way, it is important for organizations to have a vision statement that is both *inspirational* and *aspirational*. Are your staff genuinely inspired by the vision of the organization or is it just viewed as some bland words on a paper that don't really matter? Have you already achieved your vision, or is it actually something you can aspire to?

One of the key mistakes I see with organizational vision statements is that they simply say something that already exists – the vision has already been achieved. By definition, a vision should be something that is not yet so. It is something we are striving for, something we want to eventually achieve.

Once you've defined a vision that is both inspirational and aspirational, it should be front and center in all your decisions as a leader. In other words, the work of your organization and the decisions you make should support your vision. Then, when a new idea comes forth, it should always be filtered through your vision. If it supports your vision, great, go for it. If it doesn't, say no and explain your decision. This understanding will slowly start to seep into the consciousness of staff within your organization and they will begin assessing ideas in the same way.

Our vision to live in a world where everyone likes where they work will not happen overnight. But it is inspirational and aspirational and provides focus for the work we are doing. Our vision is a crucial guide not only for what we choose to do, but to help us choose what *not* to do.

We can say "no" more confidently because our vision gives us a clear reason for doing so.

REFLECTION QUESTIONS

1. What are some instances where you have (or *could* have) said no to something because it didn't support the vision of your organization?
2. In what ways is the vision of your organization inspirational and aspirational? If it isn't, what are the steps you can take to reconsider and update this vision?

PRACTICAL APPLICATION

Do an internal review of your programs, projects, and initiatives and ask yourself if they align with your organization's vision. If they don't, consider how you can alter them so they align with your vision. If that's not possible, think about whether they can be eliminated.

ADDITIONAL RESOURCES

"Vision" in *The Ordinary Leader: 10 Key Insights for Building and Leading a Thriving Organization* by Randy Grieser (ACHIEVE Publishing, 2017)

The Power of a Positive No: How to Say No and Still Get to Yes by William Ury (Bantam Dell, 2007)

13
YOU'RE HIRED

BY ERIC STUTZMAN

In a recent set of interviews for an entry-level staff position, I was asked by an applicant why I, the CEO, was involved in the interview process. They seemed surprised that someone in my position would take the time to be part of the hiring panel. At the time, I responded that hiring is such an important decision that we think senior leaders need to be involved. While I did not explain further at the time, there is much more to my answer.

As CEO, I believe getting the right people into our organization is one of my most important responsibilities. For this reason, I have directly taken part in many of our hiring decisions. More importantly, in my role as a senior leader, I have also been highly involved in creating the framework that we use for hiring. While I no longer directly participate in *every* hiring decision, there is always at least one member of our senior leadership team on the interview panel.

I also believe that leaders need to play an integral role in the hiring process rather than farming it out to an external agency or turning the entire process over to the human resources department. While recruiters and human resources often add value to the hiring process, leaders also need to be involved because they are responsible for bringing in people who will positively contribute to the organization.

Good leaders know how to hire great people, give them the right training, let them know their door is always open, and let them fly... no, really, they let them fly!

Through talking with other leaders, reading on the topic, and my experiences of participating in our own hiring process, I have learned much about what an organization can do to increase its chances of employing someone who will both do their work well *and* contribute positively to the culture of the organization. When I started with ACHIEVE, it seemed like our ability to hire successfully was only a little better than 50/50. We did not view this as good enough, so we set out to change and enhance our hiring process. Almost a decade later, I would say we are now successful approximately 80 percent of the time. By successful, I mean hiring someone who excels at their role, is excited to do the work, and contributes positively to our organizational culture over the long term. I have come to see that hiring includes the following three essential elements.

Assessing Aptitude and Skills

Fundamentally, organizations must hire people who can do the work. Most workplaces focus on finding the most skilled person with the best training, expertise, and experience to do the work. While I believe these things are important, I think a subtle shift in focus must happen for hiring to be as successful as possible. We have found that we should concentrate first on finding someone with the right *aptitudes*.

Aptitudes are areas where people have *natural* ability or inclinations – in other words, what the person is inherently good at. They are formed early in life and are based on patterned ways of thinking and relating, reinforced in our brains through repeated use. When people are asked to do tasks in areas where they have aptitude, they find learning those tasks easier than a task where they do not have aptitude. They also normally find doing those tasks rewarding or satisfying because they are working with their strengths.

By contrast, skillfulness does *not* predict whether someone will find a task or job satisfying. For instance, two people may both have the skills to follow a recipe and cook a meal, but the person who has an aptitude for making food delicious will make a better meal – *and* they will get more satisfaction from having done the work. The person who has the skill but not the aptitude will be able to read the recipe but won't derive as much satisfaction from the task, and the result will likely be okay but not great.

Practically speaking, at ACHIEVE we now orient our interview questions to try to understand what our applicants are naturally good at, what they spend time thinking about, and what they care about. This is because we want to understand how their brains work. We also ask questions about what brings them satisfaction because that is often an indicator of an area where someone has aptitude.

Assessing Values

Given the role of values in shaping how we behave, we put our values front and center during the interview process. We do this in three ways:

1. First, we build interview questions that relate to our values. For instance, we ask participants about the place or role of friendship at work and their experience related to this. We are hoping that they will say something like, "Friendships at work are really important. In my last workplace, being a friend meant ..." This question relates to our value of engagement – caring about our mission *and* each other.

2. Part way through the interview, we show the applicant our values and talk about what they mean to us and how they guide our behavior. Then we ask them to talk about what they see in our values and what these values mean to them. When we show an applicant our values, we are essentially telling

them that they are important to us and that we want our staff to be able to align with them.

3. We also specifically "test" for our values within the interview process. For example, one of our values is being receptive, meaning we are open to feedback and improvement. So, we ask a question about a time when the applicant received feedback that was hard to hear and how they responded. We also show them a list of our values that includes "receptive." Then, a little later in the interview, we gently give the candidate feedback on an element of the interview or application such as some missing information or a typo on their resume. Their responses are telling: some people get defensive and blame their proofreader, while others thank us and assure us that they will fix it as soon as they get home. Finally, we ask their references to comment on how the candidate responds to feedback. These methods frequently show us which candidate will best embody our value of receiving feedback well.

Assessing Fit

For a new employee to positively contribute to an organization, they must be able to both excel at the work *and* fit with the team. Fit refers to whether someone will relate positively to their peers in the organization. Assessing for fit does not mean looking for candidates who will look and act like everyone else on the team. In fact, we see this as detrimental to the health of the organization as we know that diversity leads to stronger organizational health and work outcomes. Instead, assessing for fit means determining whether a candidate will be able to build respectful relationships and work well with the existing team. We have learned that we should not leave assessment of fit solely to the hiring committee. Instead, we want to understand how other people in the organization experience the applicant. So, we do two things:

1. After the interview, we talk to the people in the front office who interacted with applicants as they came into the building and as they left. We ask if the applicants treated them in a friendly way and what their basic impression of them was. This tells us about how our clients or visitors may experience this person.

2. Once we have shortlisted the candidates, we then bring the top one or two back to our office for an informal opportunity to meet people and see firsthand what they would be doing in the role. Someone from the team who would be working with the candidate gives them a tour of the office and introduces them to everyone. Then they sit with the applicant and show them various aspects of the job. This gives the applicant an opportunity to see whether they would actually like the job and their potential coworkers; it also gives our team a chance to see how the potential hire responds to the work and what it's like to spend time with them. This process concludes with the leader of the interview committee asking the existing team, "What do you think it would be like to work with this person, and why?" Their answers help the hiring committee make its final decision.

When leaders involve themselves in the hiring process, they signal to others how important it is for the organization to bring on the right person. As they focus on ensuring that the organization's values are brought into the process and help assess for aptitude and fit, they increase the chance of hiring someone who will contribute positively to the organization for a long time to come.

REFLECTION QUESTIONS

1. When it comes to hiring, what information do you currently prioritize through your interview process? Are you more focused on expertise, experiences, and skills, or on aptitude, values, and fit?

2. Consider a position that you have recently hired for or one that you anticipate filling in the next year. What could you add or adjust to make your hiring process more effective?

PRACTICAL APPLICATION

Look at the list of questions that your organization uses in interviews. Evaluate which ones discover aptitude, assess fit for the team, and connect with the organization's values. Take some time to edit the questions or write new ones to make them more effective. Discuss your ideas with others who have a role in hiring.

ADDITIONAL RESOURCE

First, Break all The Rules: What the World's Greatest Managers Do Differently by Curt Coffman and Marcus Buckingham (Gallup Press, 2016)

14

BREAKING UP
IS HARD TO DO

BY RANDY GRIESER

Most of us are familiar with the collective sigh of relief that comes after a poorly performing or toxic member of the team is fired or leaves. In these situations, remaining staff are usually more than happy to pick up the former employee's tasks, and motivation and productivity often increase for the whole organization despite having one less person to do the work.

There is a lot of literature about the importance of hiring the right people for your organization, but I have noticed there is less conversation around letting people go. This is unfortunate because while I believe that a clear and thoughtful hiring process is important, I also believe that knowing when to fire someone is equally as important. One of my roles as a leader is to protect my organization's viability and culture, and sometimes this means letting go of people who don't fit.

At ACHIEVE we have a very intentional hiring process. Our interview sessions are carefully designed to focus on making sure candidates fit our culture as it is defined by our core values, and that they will do well with the tasks of the position. However, after many years of using this intentional hiring approach, sometimes we still end up getting it wrong. While I'm sure it's possible to perfect our hiring process even further, I've come to believe that there will inevitably be some hiring decisions we make that don't end up working out.

When we realize someone is not a good fit for our organization's culture or the tasks they were hired to do – and after attempts to coach, train, or discipline fail – it's time to step up and make the decision to let someone go.

I often see workplaces hold on to underperforming or disruptive employees for far too long. Intuition, performance markers, and occasionally even other employees will tell managers that this person is not working out, yet they are still slow to take action. Below are five reasons I've seen leaders give for being resistant to letting someone go.

Their Unique Skill Set Is Not Easily Replaced

Jim from accounting is just too valuable. He may be a jerk, but his expertise would really be missed if he were let go, so he is allowed to stay while others have to tiptoe around him. Despite Jim's valuable skill set, his toxic behavior negatively impacts other people's engagement and performance.

I think not letting someone go because their skill set would be missed is a poor excuse. No matter how skilled a person is, their value, and indirectly the value of others, plummets if that person is toxic to the workplace culture. As a leader, you need to remember that no one is irreplaceable – the short-term pain of firing someone who is not a good fit will be worth the long-term gain in organizational health.

They're a Nice Person

Underperforming employees aren't always indifferent or mean. Firing someone who is nice is always difficult, yet keeping someone who underperforms and does their job poorly will eventually bring the rest of the team's motivation and performance down.

In my experience as both an employee and a leader, I have seen how important it is to be surrounded by other motivated, talented, and productive people. A saying I often use in my work is "Talent motivates talent." In other words, talented people want to be surrounded by other talented individuals. As a leader, know that staff will feel the impact of a low-performing team member and that your role is to make sure teams perform at their peak – this means that *everyone* needs to be competent.

It's Too Time Consuming to Replace Them

Some managers delay firing because the hiring process can be time consuming and take staff away from other work. What those who believe this may fail to recognize is that the underperforming or disruptive employee will take more of management's time than necessary over the long term.

By not doing anything you risk alienating those employees you want to be happy and productive. Although hiring and training do require a short-term investment of energy and time, that effort pales in comparison to the ongoing requirements of managing someone who is performing poorly.

It Might Get Better

Many managers continue to believe that things will get better if the person is given yet another chance. As a leader, I do believe in second and even third chances – but eventually enough is enough.

Before letting someone go, we should first give them a chance to improve by letting them know about the impact of their behavior or performance on the team and highlighting the importance of living up to our core values. However, if their attitude and performance don't improve quickly, we should let them go. If our initial efforts to coach and train aren't paying off, simply continuing those efforts likely won't bring about change. In most cases, if a person is capable of changing, you will see changes quickly.

It Will Negatively Affect Morale

Letting someone go is not only hard for the person being fired – it can be difficult for those they work with as well. People working alongside the underperforming staff member are often shouldered with picking up their slack or dealing with their mistakes. As a result, the relief that comes with no longer having to do this often outweighs any bad feelings about that staff member being let go. This is especially true when the termination is handled with respect and care. Remember that morale is also affected when you don't let underperformers or toxic people go.

One person can have a destructive impact on your organization. If you have an employee who does not do their work at a high enough level, is indifferent about being there, whose behavior is disruptive, or who does not live by your core values, continuing their employment is an unhealthy choice.

SURVEY QUOTE
An effective leader will handle problematic employees quickly – they don't ignore or avoid the issues.

Letting these types of people stay inevitably means leadership is not addressing performance issues or holding employees accountable to the core values of the organization. This sends the wrong message to other employees, essentially showing them it's okay to underperform or not behave in the way we say everyone at the organization should behave. Over time, this will negatively affect the attitudes, engagement, and performance of the whole organization.

On the other hand, when we do let people go, we show staff that we are willing to protect our culture and have high standards for our workplace. This creates the type of organization people are proud to be a part of.

REFLECTION QUESTIONS

1. What has been your experience when you or your organization has held on to an employee too long? How did this affect you and others in your organization?
2. Which of the five reasons listed for being resistant to letting someone go is your organization at risk of relying on? What impact does this have on you and your organization? What do you need to do to set this excuse aside?

PRACTICAL APPLICATION

Within the next month, schedule a meeting with relevant leaders in your workplace and consider your history with firing or keeping underperforming or disruptive employees. Talk through each of the five reasons for being resistant to firing employees and consider how they apply to your organization. Work to develop clarity about what your process of firing is and when you will use it.

ADDITIONAL RESOURCE

Dismissing an Employee: Expert Solutions to Everyday Challenges by Harvard Business School Publishing (Harvard Business School Publishing, 2007)

15

YOUR DECISION-MAKING PROCESS MATTERS

BY ERIC STUTZMAN

"I'm so frustrated!" exclaimed the person I was speaking with. "I can't believe I even bothered to say anything at the meeting. They already knew what decision they were going to make. They just held the meeting to *pretend* like they cared about what we had to say!"

Unfortunately, I've heard this sentiment many times throughout my experiences as an organizational consultant. In this case I was working with a team of about 40 people who were contemplating a significant structural change in the workflow of their department. The leadership team held a meeting to consult the staff about what they wanted. However, after the meeting it appeared to staff that the leadership team had already made a decision, and the "consultation" process was just designed to give the illusion of collaboration in order to make staff think they had a voice. They felt as though their time had been wasted, and even worse, that the leadership team didn't really care about what they had to say.

All leaders should strive for clarity in making decisions. When leaders are not clear about the decision-making process for an issue, including who is making the decision and how, they risk creating conflict or disengaging staff. When it comes to decisions, people care deeply about transparency – they need to know what process is being used and want their expertise or opinions to be valued.

Transparency in decision-making processes directly influences our willingness to trust the results. Consider the lengths governments go to in order to ensure transparency in an election process so that the citizens trust the results. If the process is not transparent, people quickly become distrustful. By the same token, leaders should be transparent about the decisions that are made in their organizations if they want their staff to trust the decisions that affect them.

Transparency can include any number of factors, including information about who is making the decision, what data is being considered, and what process is being used. I have learned that when I make the effort to communicate as much information as I can, it puts employees' fears at ease, and they will more easily support a decision. Sometimes I'm reminded of this the hard way. Recently, a colleague and I decided to engage an external technology consultant to help us create better infrastructure. Initially, we decided to work with the consultant without discussing it with our tech team and, predictably, our decision was met with some fear and resistance. I took that as a cue to slow down, listen to the fears of my team, discuss my rationale for working with the consultant, and then bring the team alongside us as we re-engaged with the consultant. This resulted in a much happier team because they felt included in the process and had the information needed to understand the decision.

Further to transparency, people also need to understand *how* the decision is being made so that they know how to engage in the process. If a decision is being made by an individual or small committee without consultation, staff will know they don't have to think about

Transparency in decision-making processes directly influences our willingness to trust the results.

it or contribute. If a decision is being made by an individual or small committee after consultation with a wider group, staff will know they need to prepare and that their voice will be heard. And if the decision is going to be made by the wider group by voting or consensus decision-making, then staff will know that they should be prepared to invest even more in the process. Whatever the case may be, leaders should always create clear expectations about whether staff are being given information about a decision that has already been made, are being consulted prior to a decision, or if they are being asked to make a decision together.

In addition to being clear about the process they're using to make the decision, leaders may also find it valuable to say *why* that process is being used. I have found it helpful to follow a few simple rules when it comes to choosing a process. First, if the ultimate responsibility for a decision rests with an individual or small group, then they should fully own the decision and not give it to others to make, even if it is tempting to pass the responsibility. Second, if the decision affects other people, the decision maker should strongly consider consulting those who will be impacted by the decision. The bigger the impact on the group, the higher the rationale for consulting. And finally, if a decision is either the responsibility of the whole group or if wide buy-in is needed, the leader should consider using a group process such as voting or consensus decision-making.

It creates intense frustration for people when they are asked for their opinion or to provide information, only to find out or suspect that what they contributed was not actually considered in the final decision. When decision makers consult others, they must be prepared to take into account what they hear. This does not mean that they need to agree with every voice in the consultation process but that they must value it. After a decision is made, the decision maker needs to communicate the result of the decision, what they considered, and, if possible, why they went with the option they chose. This gives those who were involved in consultation a sense of closure, and it communicates that their input was valued. I have seen that most people will go along with a decision without significant complaint as long as their contribution was considered.

I have guided many groups through decision-making processes over the years. Through my experiences, I have learned that the best decision-making involves transparency, clear process, and valuing what people contribute during consultation. When people believe the process is transparent and clear, and that they were listened to, they are more likely to trust the results. And trust makes it possible to proceed with the outcome of the decision and do the work.

REFLECTION QUESTIONS

1. Think about a time when a decision-making process was not clear. How did it affect you and other people? What could the leader have done to make the process better?
2. How intentional are you and other leaders in your organization about your decision-making processes? What could you do to make your practices stronger?

PRACTICAL APPLICATION

Looking ahead, consider what kind of decisions you will need to make in the coming weeks. Think about which decisions require transparent communication, which would benefit from consultation, and where a clearly understood process is imperative. Make a plan to incorporate the ideas from this insight in your next decision-making process.

ADDITIONAL RESOURCE

Facilitator's Guide to Participatory Decision-Making by Sam Kaner, Lenny Lind, Catherine Toldi, Sarah Fisk, and Duane Berger (Jossey-Bass, 2014)

16
TAKE THE TIME
TO LISTEN

BY WENDY LOEWEN

As a result of failing to listen carefully, my husband and I missed my dear friend's wedding. The day of the event, I excitedly got ready, packed our gift in the car, and we headed out. My husband was adamant that we should not be late, so we left early. We arrived at an empty parking lot to which I said, "Look, we're the first ones here!" We made our way inside the church only to be informed by the janitor that everyone had already left and were on their way across town to the reception. It turned out that the wedding was at 12:30 p.m., not 2:30 p.m. I was mortified, and my husband was annoyed.

As I played back the conversation when my friend told me about her wedding plans, it became clear that I had not really listened when she said the time, and I never bothered to double-check. When my husband asked me when the wedding was, I told him 2:30. In my mind, that's when the wedding was, and I was so sure I was right. As I began thinking and writing about the importance of listening in our roles as leaders, this memory jumped into my mind. It's easy for leaders to miss things and make poor decisions when we do not take the time to *truly listen*.

Most leaders spend a lot of time thinking about how we communicate and know how crucial it is. We read and reread our emails, spend hours planning for presentations with clients, consider and then reconsider how to pitch a product, or think and rethink how to best share information at a staff meeting. It is easy to think that communicating as a leader is primarily giving out information. However, effective communication includes a two-way exchange of both giving *and* receiving information.

Often in my coaching practice, clients will approach me because they want to learn to communicate better. When I ask them specifically what they would like to work on, they often say they would like to be able to articulate their ideas well, increase their level of assertiveness, and speak with more clarity. These are all valuable communication skills to have, but we need to pair them with an ability to listen well if we are to be effective leaders.

SURVEY STATISTICS

When survey respondents were asked to describe the attributes of a great leader, 15 significant characteristics emerged in their long-form answers. We were struck that the most frequently cited characteristic of a great leader was being a *good listener.* Some form of the word *listen* was noted 299 times, followed by *communicate*, with 240 mentions. *You will find a list of these characteristics in the Survey Analysis on page 262.*

As a leader it can be hard to know what our staff are thinking, what their ideas for improvement are, or how to support them, unless we really take the time to listen. When we listen to others it shows that we respect their ideas while building trust, expanding our perspective, and ensuring we have the necessary information to give direction or provide guidance. I have found some practices that have been helpful for me as I strive to be a better listener both in my personal life and as a leader.

Be Humble

Being a good listener requires us to be humble, no matter the situation or circumstance. It is helpful for us to remember that each person on our team is an expert in something we are not; we don't always have all the answers and they may have valuable information that we have missed. With this approach, you'll find that you *want* to listen to what the people around you have to contribute so you can learn from them. Being humble prepares us to be genuinely interested in people, assume the best about them, and demonstrate that we sincerely desire to understand their point of view.

Ask Questions

Our role in listening is to gain a deeper understanding, withhold judgment, and refrain from adding our insightful comments unless asked. Some of us have the tendency to interrupt and say what is on our mind. While listening happens mostly through hearing, we can demonstrate that we are listening with our voices by asking clarifying questions. When someone comes to us for advice, asking questions will also help us gain a more complete perspective. In addition, I have found that a powerful way to draw people out is to pair questioning with encouragements to speak, such as "Tell me more ..." This lets the other person know that we are interested and are giving them an opportunity to open up. It also provides the opportunity for people to become their own problem solvers, as good questions will help them better be able to think through the issue or problem they are facing.

Remain Present

When the people we lead are sharing ideas or responding to something we've asked, we need to fully listen – and *then* respond. We need to be aware of when our thoughts wander to unrelated things or, instead of listening, when we begin thinking of what we want to say in response. It takes a lot of determination and concentration to stay focused. If our thoughts wander, we should ask for clarification and get back to paying attention. Always remember that when people share their ideas, experiences, or emotions, they are giving us something of themselves and we should fully receive it.

One way that I remain present is by challenging myself to paraphrase or summarize what the other person has said, either out loud or in my head. This keeps me engaged, increases my interest in what they are saying, raises my level of empathy, and I gain a clear picture of what they are really trying to communicate. When I paraphrase out loud, it also shows the other person that I am paying attention, that what they have to say matters, and that I have heard what they are saying.

Leaders who do not listen often find that the people around them have nothing to say, causing them to lose valuable input as a result. When we listen well, we hear a diversity of perspectives that can ultimately lead to more creative solutions and approaches to the issues we face. Every one of our staff members should know that we are interested in their thoughts, ideas, and opinions. They should anticipate that we will prioritize taking the time to actively engage in listening to them. When we intentionally follow the simple listening tips above, we can build our listening skills and become better leaders who are able to make well-considered decisions, provide helpful guidance, and empower our teams to be problem solvers.

REFLECTION QUESTIONS

1. As an employee, when have you felt really listened to by a manager? What were the signs and cues that your manager was genuinely interested in what you had to say? What did they do that made them effective at listening? In what ways do you or do you not do these same things?

2. Consider how much time you typically spend preparing for the parts of your job that rely heavily on your verbal presenting skills. In what ways could you spend the same amount of time strengthening your listening skills?

PRACTICAL APPLICATION

Over the next week, pay attention to the balance of how much you talk versus how much you listen. Also consider whether you are giving out more answers than you are asking questions. When someone approaches you with a problem or to share something personal, intentionally and genuinely pay attention to them as they speak. Seek to be curious, stay present, and then follow up with a question.

ADDITIONAL RESOURCE

Humble Inquiry: The Gentle Art of Asking Instead of Telling by Edgar H. Schein (Berrett-Koehler Publishers, 2013)

17

SUPPORT MENTAL HEALTH AT WORK

BY RANDY GRIESER

Prior to founding ACHIEVE, I worked as a social worker in the field of mental health – both in hospital settings and in the community, providing support to those living with mental health concerns. My role in supporting people's recovery would sometimes involve conversations with their employers about ways to best support their return to work.

I was often struck by how different employers responded to these conversations. Some were empathetic and supportive of the employee, while others were indifferent and unsupportive. In these latter situations, return-to-work attempts were often unsuccessful. Throughout my time working in this role and engaging with various employers, I quickly learned that organizations and leaders can either contribute positively or negatively to a person's mental health.

Organizations that don't give priority to supporting the mental health of their employees are being shortsighted. I believe first and foremost that workplaces should care about mental health because, simply put, it is the right thing to do. As a society, as workplaces, and as individuals who are part of the larger community, we *should* care about and support those who experience mental health concerns because it's the kind and humane way to behave. And it's what we would want and need when we are impacted by mental health concerns. But if that isn't

Workplaces should care about mental health because, simply put, it is the right thing to do.

enough, there are also significant organizational costs that can come when mental health is not supported by an organization, including loss of productivity, absenteeism, presenteeism (at work physically, but not mentally focused), and turnover.[1] In short, organizations that do the right thing by investing in the mental health and well-being of employees will be richly rewarded with sustainable workplace performance and productivity.

Mental health concerns either directly or indirectly affect all people at some point in their lives – either personally or through a family member, friend, or colleague. The sheer number of people affected by mental illness – one in seven[2] – means that mental health is an issue that impacts almost every workplace. Given the prevalence of mental illness, it is important that organizations have both the will and capacity to support mental health, because early identification and support typically lead to continued productivity and retention of employees. With the right support, people with mental health concerns can thrive in the workplace.

One of the best ways to support mental health in the workplace is to be proactive and ensure that you are providing a safe and healthy workplace for staff. When this does not occur, the impacts of stress and conflict lead to the risk of burnout and contribute to mental health concerns. To be proactive, you should work to ensure your organization is competent in the following six areas.

Healthy Workplace Culture

People spend so much time at work that the culture of an organization can't help but impact their mental health – the healthier the culture, the more supportive it will be for the individual. Be intentional about creating a workplace where employees feel safe, supported, and respected. *Read Focus on Culture, Not Perks on page 163 for more information on creating healthy workplace cultures.*

Formal Policies
Ensure your policies and reporting procedures around things like respect, harassment, and discrimination in the workplace are clear and consistently applied and enforced. Clearly articulate the importance of using vacation and sick days so that people take breaks. Consider if your staff orientation to these policies is adequate.

Accessibility of Services and Programs
If counselling services are a part of benefits, ensure that staff understand how to access them. Become aware of community resources that may be helpful, work to let staff know about them, and normalize access to these services.

Training and Development
Offer training to both employees and managers in mental health awareness and support. The more educated people are about mental health, the more likely they will be to help each other and feel comfortable seeking help when they need it. Be sure your leadership development training program fosters leaders who are caring and empathetic.

Management of Psychological Hazards
Exposure to psychological hazards like toxic conflict, bullying, and harassment can negatively impact a person's mental health. Ensure managers know how to deal with these issues by providing them with adequate training and support. Then make sure staff know who to speak with if they are experiencing any of these issues.

Leading by Example

Leadership should be visibly and actively engaged in supporting mental health. One way to do this is to normalize conversations around mental health. When leaders are comfortable and proactive in having open conversations around mental health, it shows staff that it's safe to talk about it at work.

Investing in mental health is investing in our best asset – our staff. When we invest in our staff and their well-being, they are in a better position to support the mission and vision of our organization. But when people are not mentally healthy, it's next to impossible to function at a high level. When we work to support mental health concerns in the workplace, it benefits both employees and the organization.

REFLECTION QUESTIONS

1. What have been the positive and/or negative experiences you have had or observed around organizational responses to mental health in the workplace?
2. How does your organization provide support for mental health? Which of the six areas above could use more attention from you and other leaders in your organization?

PRACTICAL APPLICATION

The next time you have a staff meeting, start to reduce stigma around mental health in the workplace by talking about it. Lead by example and show that it's okay to talk about mental health by sharing a personal experience or showing a video promoting mental health awareness.

ADDITIONAL RESOURCE

Mental Health and Wellbeing in the Workplace: A Practical Guide for Employers and Employees by Gill Hasson and Donna Butler (Capstone, 2020)

18

HOW TO LEAD A DIFFICULT PERSON

BY ERIC STUTZMAN

Most people are easy to lead. However, many of us will eventually come across someone in our career that we find difficult. I recently sat down with a leader who immediately launched into her frustrations about an employee she was finding difficult to manage. "He's just so reactive!" she said. I felt my stomach churn because I could relate to her frustration and feelings of helplessness. She followed up by saying, "I just want him to change." Although I empathized with that desire, I challenged her on her thinking given what I have learned about difficult relationships.

To work with a person we find difficult, we must start with a focus on ourselves – *not* the other person. Here's why: How we *think* about someone has a direct bearing on how we *act* toward them. How we act influences how the other person experiences us. And their experience of us affects how they then (re)act toward us.

To work with a person we find difficult, we must start with a focus on ourselves – not the other person.

For instance, the leader I was meeting with told me that her difficult person was "reactive," "stubborn," and "standoffish." In labeling him that way, she gave herself a lens that colored the way she saw all of her employee's actions. If he didn't greet her in the morning, it became further evidence that the employee was standoffish. If he questioned a new assignment, it became further evidence that he was "stubborn."

Furthermore, this leader's beliefs about her employee created a *negative reinforcement loop*. Given that she believed her employee was standoffish, she stopped trying to make small talk with him. For this leader to start with herself, it would mean considering how her own withdrawal may be creating the conditions for the employee to act in ways that reinforce her views that he is standoffish.

Negative Reinforcement Loop

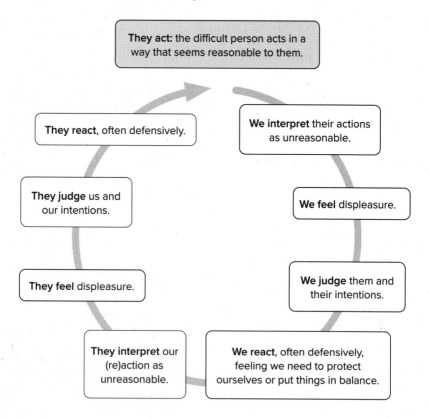

Over time I have learned that to prevent these negative reinforcement loops, it is essential to consider the way I am thinking. When we change the way we think, we can change our actions and get different results from those around us.

For example, if I say to myself (or others) that someone is passive aggressive, I need to realize that I have essentially judged their character. Judging character makes it easy for us to write someone off because we know that it is hard to change someone's character. When we judge someone's character, the natural next step is to build defensive strategies to guard against their negative personality trait. This does not lead to open conversations.

Another problem with judging someone's character is that our beliefs influence what we say or do. For instance, if we *believe* that someone is passive aggressive, then we might confront them with something that sounds like, "You are passive aggressive, and you need to change." And that will almost certainly generate a defensive response from them.

The alternative to judging character is to focus on specific behaviors and their impact on us. Focusing on behavior means noticing what someone is doing in an objective way, rather than our interpretation of what they are doing and our judgment of their character. When we focus on what they do and the impact of their behavior, we have a place to start a conversation that is based on observable facts. Starting a conversation with a focus on what has happened (observable facts) and the impact of those actions creates more openness than a conversation that starts with a negative judgment of someone's character. The natural next step in a conversation that starts this way is to discuss whether the impact was what the other person intended.

In the training work that I do, I often ask rooms full of people to raise their hands if they think they are a reasonable person. As you might expect, most people raise their hand. Next, I ask everyone to raise their hand if they think they are a difficult person. And of course, most people don't raise their hand because they don't think of themselves as difficult. What this tells us is that *everyone* sees themselves as reasonable, including the people we find difficult.

If a difficult person views their behavior as reasonable, then our task is to begin to wonder how their behavior makes sense in their mind. Wondering motivates us to ask questions that will help us enter into a productive conversation with the other person. It means shifting from judgment (*They're passive-aggressive!*) to curiosity (*I wonder why they aren't feeling safe enough to directly tell me what they think?*). Curiosity gives us the ability to start a conversation with a question and to listen. It moves us toward empathy.

As leaders, we need to shift our thinking and suspend our judgment in order to have more productive conversations with people we find difficult. However, given a leader's power within a workplace, we also need focus on creating a safe conversational space for the other person.

Safe conversations are truthful and open, but in careful ways. I have often heard leaders use phrases like, "Can I be brutally honest?" When I hear this, I cringe because I don't believe *brutality* has a place in our world. Instead, leaders must be honest in safe ways that protect the dignity of the person they find difficult. Safe honesty focuses on behaviors and impacts, not character judgments – and it shows care for the dignity of each person.

It is also important to maintain our focus on the pattern of behavior that is leading to negative impacts. One of the easiest mistakes to make is to lose sight of the pattern and focus on the most recent incident(s). Focusing on the most recent incident(s) does not help the other person see how serious this is for us. They may think it is an isolated thing that is easily explained by what was happening that day, an exception to the rule. Instead, we need to remember to bring the conversation back to the pattern we have experienced.

Here's an example of how the leader in my earlier example might focus on a pattern: "I've noticed that over the last several months when staff are connecting, like at the coffee machine at the start of the day, you walk by without greeting them – even when someone calls out a 'Good morning.' When I am a part of the group, it leaves me feeling ignored and wondering what is going on. I'd like to hear what is happening for you and try to figure out what we can do differently."

Dealing with difficult people can be a challenge for any leader, but when we take time to understand ourselves *and* understand the other person, we create a foundation for respectful conversations that can help change negative behavior patterns. This kind of leadership creates a positive loop that strengthens our relationships for the future.

REFLECTION QUESTIONS

1. What is your experience with leading someone you find difficult? What have you learned about what works or what doesn't work when it comes to changing the relationship dynamic with them?
2. How do the suggestions in this insight resonate with your own experiences? What could you add to your approach the next time you need to talk with someone you find difficult?

PRACTICAL APPLICATION

Consider someone you find difficult in your workplace. Think about ways you might have judged their character with words like *lazy*, *disengaged*, or *reactive*. Write your words down. Beside each word, describe the other person's actions in factual ways and note the impact it has had on you or others. Plan to connect with this person and have a conversation where you ask about the pattern, try to understand their perspective, and work to find a new way of interacting.

ADDITIONAL RESOURCE

Crucial Conversations: Tools for Talking When Stakes Are High by Kerry Patterson, Joseph Grenny, Ron McMillan, and Al Switzler (McGraw-Hill Education, 2011)

19
REMOVE BARRIERS
TO ENGAGEMENT

BY WENDY LOEWEN

Several years ago, I worked with an organization that was struggling with low employee engagement. After years of success, this organization was now faced with disgruntled employees, increasing rates of absenteeism, and clients who were beginning to complain that they were not getting the quality of service they had come to expect.

Knowing that something needed to be done and hoping for a quick fix, management removed several of the "bad apples," thinking that would improve the situation. But when morale and engagement didn't improve, they got rid of a few more. Then, to the organization's surprise, several valued staff opted to leave on their own; employee engagement had plummeted. Not to be defeated, the organization's leadership team tried to put a positive spin on their predicament. They reframed the situation as a fresh start and tried to be optimistic.

The vacant positions were filled, which initially brought a burst of energy. But they soon found themselves back where they had been before – morale was again low, and employees were disengaged. Like many leaders are tempted to do, this organization's leadership team put the blame for disengagement squarely onto the shoulders of their employees rather than taking a look at how they were leading.

When trying to make sense of low levels of engagement, I've often heard leaders make statements like, "There is a lack of talent to draw from" or "This generation just doesn't know how to work!" Some leaders go further and see employee disengagement as a sign of laziness, apathy, or even insubordination. They view it as a bad habit that must be broken and often resort to forceful command-and-control strategies, which are not only ineffective at increasing employee engagement but can also cause employees to retreat further.

A common theme I've observed when consulting with organizations is that leadership is often so focused on what they see their employees doing (or not doing) that they fail to look at the way they are leading and how that may be creating barriers to engagement. For example, in the case of the organization above, I learned that one of the leaders routinely criticized and yelled at her staff members, which led to a situation where staff dreaded coming to work each day. This leader was totally unaware of how her own behavior was creating the disengagement in her employees that she wanted me to help fix. One of the other leaders in this organization was so disorganized that staff routinely spent large chunks of time just trying to figure out what to do, creating frustration and a sense that their work was pointless.

In my own leadership work at ACHIEVE, I have come to recognize that I play a large role in supporting employee engagement and that there have been times when I have inadvertently been responsible for hindering it. I have learned that when one of my team struggles with engagement, I need to reflect on my role in the situation, consider what might be going on for the person, and then think about what I can influence.

Leadership is often so focused on what they see their employees doing (or not doing) that they fail to look at the way they are leading and how that may be creating barriers to engagement.

To prompt my reflection, I have created a list of questions to ask myself when I see someone not engaging fully with their work. These questions allow me to see the barriers that I may be responsible for and then help me consider what my course of action should be:

- Have I clearly communicated to the employee *what* they are supposed to do?
- Have I communicated *why* they should do it?
- Have I set clear expectations?
- Have I positively affirmed and validated their good work?
- Have I identified the impact of their poor performance?
- Have I ensured that they are capable of doing the work?

If I can't answer the questions in the affirmative or am unsure of how the employee themselves might answer the question, I have a direct conversation with them. When I have had such conversations with our own staff and facilitated them in my consulting work, I repeatedly hear that most employees *want* to do better, give more, and make their organization successful, and that sometimes leaders have failed to own up to their part in the problem.

In addition to reflecting on the questions above, we should also be mindful that there are sometimes organizational factors that prevent our staff from doing good work and they may face challenges that are beyond their control. One of our responsibilities is to be vigilant in assessing what factors outside of the employee's control might be contributing to disengagement and how we can address them. There are a few that we should be aware of and work to overcome.

Inadequate Resources

If we expect quality work, we need to provide adequate resources. This includes enough time to do good work as well as the necessary material resources and tools to complete tasks. In our evolving work environment, we should regularly be assessing if we are outfitting our staff for success and asking what additional resources they would find helpful.

Unclear Procedures

Carefully looking at our workflow processes will help us identify where our procedures or systems may be frustrating employees and hindering engagement. Asking what workflow issues are slowing them down may alert us to areas of improvement. "This is how it's always been done" is not a good reason to continue with inefficient procedures.

Lack of Ongoing Training

Some organizations feel that ongoing training is an unnecessary expense. However, investing in training is a sure way to make the most of the talents of your staff and help them feel like they are growing. Training should not only be delivered during onboarding but should be an ongoing commitment to investing in our staff and our organization's long-term success. Keep checking in with your staff about how you can support them to keep their skills up to date.

Supports to Employee Engagement

When our employees are engaged, we will naturally see great customer service and innovation, and our organizational goals will be met. Our goal as leaders should be to eliminate barriers to engagement as we strive to keep our organization performing at its best.

As leaders, we can choose to recognize our role in supporting engagement by focusing on asking thoughtful questions of ourselves and our staff, and then listening to what we discern. When we do this and also ensure that we are paying attention to any factors that may be beyond their control, we create the conditions for our staff to engage in their work.

REFLECTION QUESTIONS

1. Think about a time when you were deeply engaged in your work and exceeded expectations. What led to your exceptional performance? What role did the leaders around you play? What does this tell you about the role of leadership in supporting a culture of engagement?
2. Which of your employees shows a lack of engagement? What factors may be contributing to this? What could you do to help them engage more fully in their work?

PRACTICAL APPLICATION

As you interact with your team members this week, consider what barriers to engagement they might be experiencing in their role and what you can do to help address them. Ask questions to really understand their work experience and what they need from you to perform at their best. Ask them if they have the right resources, if there are ways to improve a process or procedure that impacts their work, and if there are areas in which they would like additional training. Then trust their perspective and provide them with the supports they have identified.

ADDITIONAL RESOURCES

The Truth About Employee Engagement: A Fable About Addressing the Three Root Causes of Misery by Patrick Lencioni (Jossey-Bass, 2015)

TED Talk: "The Puzzle of Motivation" by Dan Pink

20
WHAT MY CONCUSSION TAUGHT ME ABOUT RESILIENCE

BY RANDY GRIESER

Although I'm physically fit and love mountain biking, I "retired" from it earlier this year. For most of my adult life, mountain biking has been my favorite hobby. Unfortunately, it has not been without consequences – five years ago I hit my head on a tree while riding my bike. This incident has had an impact on my life ever since.

After hitting my head, I immediately felt that something was wrong. A few days went by after the incident, and I still didn't feel good. In addition to feeling lethargic, I was having difficulty thinking clearly and processing information. About a week after the incident, a strange new symptom started – I became perpetually dizzy. While my other symptoms have lessened over the years (although not completely), this sense of dizziness has become a constant in my life, even now as I write this paragraph.

Despite the chronic nature of my symptoms, for years I've been focused on achieving a full recovery. No matter how slow or incremental my improvements were, I could see and feel them over a several-month period. As part of my recovery plan, health professionals encouraged me to work toward my goal of mountain biking again. They and I envisioned a full recovery where I could enjoy all the activities that I took part in prior to my concussion. Lately, however, I have been stuck and have even regressed *because* of mountain biking.

Twice this past year, I have had setbacks: one came after falling hard on my side, which resulted in whiplash (I didn't even hit my head); another happened after a light hit to my head on a small branch. Years earlier I would have felt no effect from these incidents, but now in my more fragile state, any little bump to my head or jolt to my body can cause my symptoms to worsen. After several years of trying to maintain my mountain biking hobby, it became clear that I needed to turn to a safer activity for exercise – so I've started running.

The fact that I'm now running surprises those closest to me because I've always disliked it. However, I've embraced the change and the challenge – I'm reading about running, working on goals to get better, and even investing in the right clothing and gadgets to help me be a better runner. In quick order, I've shifted from being a mountain biker to being a runner. I do miss mountain biking, but I've accepted my circumstances and have adapted.

What Is Resilience?

I remember the first thing someone said to me after hearing my concussion story and subsequent challenges: "Wow. Randy, you are really resilient." The notion of me being resilient caught me by surprise – I hadn't thought of my experience and new reality as a story of resilience. One of the common themes I've found in most resilient people is that they don't initially think of themselves that way. They are too busy living life – despite whatever circumstances they find themselves in – to consider themselves resilient.

I also initially struggled to think of myself as resilient because I've always felt there are far too many people with more significant struggles than my own. Clearly, I don't own the market on adversity, and my understanding of it doesn't merely come from my personal experience – it also comes from the various stories of hardship and resilience that surround me.

The definition of resilience is "an ability to recover from or adjust easily to misfortune or change."[1] As I thought and read more about resilience, I started to embrace my own story. For me, resilience means going on *in spite of* – it is about being able to persevere in the face of adversity. Resilience requires acceptance of a "new normal" and a willingness and ability to adapt. Those who are resilient get up, move on, and continue living – often in less-than-ideal circumstances, and sometimes with significant limitations.

Acceptance and Adaptation Are Key to Resilience

A key attribute of all resilient people is that they have accepted their situation and adapted to their difficult circumstances. For me this meant transitioning from being a mountain biker to a runner. I've also been forced to adapt how I work as a result of my ongoing symptoms because I don't have the energy I used to.

I have always been a driven and productive person, so much so that these values have become part of my core identify. And while my drive and ability to remain productive are still intact, they're at a far lower level since my concussion. I simply can't work at the intensity I used to, both because of lower energy levels and because working on a computer makes my symptoms worse.

I have adapted to this reality by changing how I think about productivity. Being productive is less about how long I work or how many things I get done, and more about *what* I get done. I now choose to focus most of my energy on meaningful and important tasks (like this book) instead of the multitude of less important items that used to fill my to-do list. I've learned that while I don't have control over how many things I can accomplish in any given day, I do have control over where I focus my energy.

Resilience requires acceptance of a "new normal" and a willingness and ability to adapt.

What Makes an Organization Resilient?

What I have learned about resilience through my own story also applies to organizations. When faced with challenges and difficulties – whether they're financial, legal, environmental, or otherwise – an organization's survival and ability to persevere is dependent on its members' *acceptance* of the situation and willingness and ability to *adapt.*

Organizations that approach difficult challenges with an attitude of "Let's just wait it out" are not accepting their new reality. They are instead putting their heads in the sand and denying that things have changed. Instead of innovating and adapting, they are stuck and at risk of not surviving. The first thing that resilient organizations need to embrace is *acceptance* of whatever situation they find themselves in.

The second thing they must do is *adapt.* Like individuals, a common theme among resilient organizations is that they don't think of themselves as resilient – they are too busy working and innovating despite whatever circumstance they find themselves in. *Going on in spite of* is key for any organization's survival. Regardless of what difficult situation you find yourself in, keep moving forward. Don't give up or just wait for things to get better.

At both a personal and organizational level, resilience is critical for achieving the best results you can in spite of setbacks or limitations. Always remember that no matter our circumstances and despite our struggles, we still have the freedom to choose – freedom to choose our attitude, freedom to choose how we respond to our circumstances, and freedom to choose what we do next.

REFLECTION QUESTIONS

1. What examples of resilience have you seen at both the personal and organizational levels?
2. Consider the last difficult challenge or circumstance your organization faced. How did you and other leaders approach the situation? In what ways did you or did you not show *acceptance*? In what ways did you or did you not *adapt*? What have you learned that you will apply to future challenges?

PRACTICAL APPLICATION

Carefully consider the circumstances your organization currently finds itself in. This could be anything from being understaffed to experiencing a natural disaster that has affected your organization. Work on first accepting your circumstances, and then look for ways you can adapt and address the situation.

ADDITIONAL RESOURCE

Option B: Facing Adversity, Building Resilience, and Finding Joy by Sheryl Sandberg and Adam Grant (Knopf, 2017)

21
THE SECRET TO
BUILDING TRUST

BY ERIC STUTZMAN

In search of some writing inspiration one afternoon, I went for a walk to our neighborhood coffee shop. While I was waiting for my coffee, the barista asked what I was up to that day. I told him I was working on an article about workplace culture and leadership. Then I asked him what he thought made a great workplace. Without missing a beat, he replied: "Trust, both with your coworkers and your leaders. Also, kindness, gentleness, and self-control – especially in leadership."

Curious about his response, I asked him what he thought was the secret to building trust. He paused and was deep in thought when his coworker jumped in and said, "Trust is the one thing that cannot be demanded – it must be earned."

My barista then replied, "I'll have to keep thinking about where trust comes from, but for now I'd say that when my leader cares about me, when they show kindness, gentleness, and self-control, I'm more likely to trust them."

I agree that trust can't be demanded, but the first barista's statement – "Also, kindness, gentleness, and self-control" – really piqued my interest. It was different from what I often hear. As I thought about our conversation on my walk back to the office, it occurred to me that this list creates the conditions for trust to emerge.

Kindness, gentleness, and self-control are aspects of our character as well as intentional choices.

I think it's worth asking: What does it mean to act with kindness, gentleness, and self-control, and how does that relate to creating trust in leadership?

Kindness means that you care about the well-being of others. It means you consider how your actions will affect people. It means that you are showing empathy.

Gentleness means you try not to cause others pain. It means you consider how your actions as a leader could cause harm to other people. If you are gentle, you consider how each person is vulnerable and may make mistakes, and you act in ways that support their growth and security.

Self-control means you process and regulate your emotions so that you can *act thoughtfully* rather than *react* without considering the impact of your actions. It means you know your triggers and have learned to pause between stimulus and response so that you choose actions that are kind and gentle.

Kindness, gentleness, and self-control are aspects of our character as well as intentional *choices*. Taken together, these qualities and the choices that come from them demonstrate care to our employees. And when we show care to our employees, we create the conditions for trust to emerge.

As part of the research for our book, *The Culture Question*, my co-authors and I surveyed approximately 2,400 people on the topic of workplace culture. Of all the links we found in our survey, the strongest was between these two statements: "I trust my leader" and "My leader cares about me as a person."[1] Then, in the research for this book, we found the same result: the two most closely linked concepts were caring leadership and trust between leaders and staff. If someone responded that their leader cares about them as a person, they were very likely to also say that they trust their leader. Demonstrating care and developing trust go hand in hand.

SURVEY STATISTICS

Nearly all respondents (94 percent) who reported that there are high levels of trust between staff and leaders indicated that leaders at their organization demonstrate care for their staff. Almost no respondents reported high levels of trust in organizations where leaders do not demonstrate care.

This makes a lot of sense when you consider the opposite – if your boss is uncaring and does not exhibit kindness, gentleness, and self-control – you will be unlikely to trust them or think you have a great place to work.

Many of us are placed in management positions because we are good at the technical aspects of our jobs. When we take on our roles, we naturally focus on what we are good at, which is the work itself. We might be tempted to try to gain the trust of our teams through demonstrating our competence, but therein lies a problem – while technical competence is valuable, it rarely builds relational trust because the focus is on the person demonstrating competence. By contrast, demonstrating care puts the focus on the person who receives the care. As leaders, we must realize that our staff need us to balance our competence with demonstrating care for their interests. Caring leadership builds the trust we need to communicate well and work together effectively.

I don't believe that demonstrating care to the people you lead is difficult. However, like all leadership practices, we can get better at it with focused effort. Although kindness, gentleness, and self-control are attributes of character, they can be nurtured in ourselves with intentionality. Here are a few thoughts on how to demonstrate care.

Act with Kindness

Consider whether your actions are building up your staff or doing the opposite. Speak positively about the people you lead and do good things for them. Take an interest in your employees' personal lives and interests – ask about those things occasionally and acknowledge their experiences.

Act with Gentleness

When you face a tough conversation with a colleague, consider ways to support the person and their dignity while communicating truthfully about whatever the problem might be. Gentleness means that you listen before acting.

Act with Self-Control

The impact of your words will be amplified by virtue of your leadership position. So, pay attention to your frustration levels and your triggers. Learn to breathe deeply and assume the best in others. Doing both will help you approach people in ways that are thoughtful and will take the negative charge out of your words and tone.

There have been times in my career when I've had leaders whose approach to leadership embodied kindness, gentleness, and self-control, and as a result they earned my trust and admiration. They help to remind me that, as a leader, when I show that I care, I create the conditions for trust to emerge in our work relationships.

REFLECTION QUESTIONS

1. Consider the leaders you have trusted the most. How would you describe their character? What concrete actions either created or reinforced your trust for that leader?

2. What would happen if you had a conversation with other leaders in your workplace about demonstrating care to your employees? How could you talk about kindness, gentleness, and self-control as these qualities relate to caring leadership?

PRACTICAL APPLICATION

Over the coming week, be intentional about creating the conditions for trust in your workplace. Plan three ways that you will demonstrate care to your staff. Then watch for the ways in which this transforms your workplace environment for the better.

ADDITIONAL RESOURCE

Leaders Eat Last: Why Some Teams Pull Together and Others Don't by Simon Sinek (Portfolio, 2017)

22

COACHING IS A
CATALYST FOR CHANGE

BY WENDY LOEWEN

My son is passionate about science. This weekend he was talking about his first university chemistry course and enthusiastically drew graphs as he described to me how a catalyst works. He explained that a catalyst is a substance that speeds up a chemical change. The change happens not because more heat or pressure is applied, but because the catalyst creates the *right conditions for change to occur*. As he described this phenomenon, I couldn't help but think that, as a leader, one of my primary roles is to be a catalyst for the growth and development of others.

Over the years I have encountered leaders who think that to create change they need to apply more force, more reasons, or more pressure. They act as if people are objects that can be pushed, pulled, or prodded – like a table you move from one end of the room to the other.

My experience has been that people don't typically respond well to being pushed, regardless of how well thought-out the leader's reasons, facts, figures, or ultimatums are. Often their reaction is to push back, argue, or internally find a rationale to oppose. They think of all the reasons they *don't* want to do what the leader hopes for, digging in their heels until the leader feels stuck. Alternatively, they may simply give in to the pressure and comply. This may result in them internalizing resentment or anger – and this damages both personal and team well-being.

Early on in my current leadership role, I was struggling with how to move forward on an important project. I sent a quick message explaining the issue to Eric, our CEO, and his response was that he was more than willing to help me think through the problem. He asked questions and helped me identify the root of the issue, encouraged me to explore options, offered his perspective, and then we mapped out some goals together. A few weeks later, he checked in to see how things were going. The conversation was a catalyst both for me to find possible solutions to the problem and for facilitating my own learning.

This interaction helped me clarify my understanding of what kind of leader I wanted to be – a leader like Eric, who draws on people's strengths and helps them figure out their next steps. I don't want to be the kind of leader who tells others what to do when they are struggling with something – I'd rather act as a catalyst for learning.

One of my favorite ACHIEVE workshops to facilitate is Coaching Strategies for Leaders because I believe that leaders can have a long-term impact on employees through coaching. Coaching encourages people to explore options and build on their own capacity. A coach becomes the catalyst for change. Coaching, however, is often misunderstood.

The word *coach* has the following definitions: "a horse drawn carriage"; "a railway car"; or "one who instructs others." At first glance, the third definition may seem like it's the most relevant to coaching for leaders, but the first two are more in line with what true coaching is about – the *journey*. Coaching is a vehicle to move people along in the right direction rather than telling them what to do.

Coaching is knowing when to share your knowledge and expertise – and when not to. Both have a place in creating successful organizations. It's about drawing out the best in people, and good coaching requires leaders to build on the skills of others, allowing them to bring their unique gifts to the organization.

*A great leader knows the balance between when and how to "push"
a staff member and when and how to guide and coach them, so they
feel empowered to challenge themselves.*

I believe that change and growth are longer lasting and deeper when the goals and steps involved come from the individual rather than from an outside force or authority figure. It struck me that Eric didn't tell me what to do, but rather asked questions to help me find the direction for myself. Sometimes you may be approached for guidance; other times you may want to approach an employee when you see they might need some added support. Either way, the following five-step framework can be used to guide conversations as you coach employees and act as a catalyst who helps them to build on their strengths.

1. Help Identify the Issue

It is helpful to clearly identify the issue that you are trying to solve. Verbally acknowledge the value in discussing and working through the problem together. Focus on providing a supportive message and keep the conversation informal. Ask questions to clarify the issue or situation.

2. Listen to Their Perspective

Ask the person to share their thoughts on the matter. Ask about what they are noticing and why they think it is important to address. Also help them consider what they have already tried. This will help you decide what your response should be and what you will say next. It is important to summarize what they have said so they can hear their own thoughts in someone else's words.

3. Provide Your Views

If you have dealt with a similar issue or situation, it may be helpful to share your experience and what you have tried and found to be helpful. This is not meant to direct their actions but to expand their thinking on the issue.

4. Develop Goals Together

Explore what they think their options are and the possible outcomes for each. Be sure to discuss any barriers to their goals and what support or training may be necessary to meet them. Make sure you communicate that you believe in their ability to address the issue.

5. Follow Up

This is an easy step to overlook, but to have a long-term impact you will need to plan a follow-up meeting. Schedule a time to check in and remember that more than one follow-up meeting may be needed. When you meet, be sure to review the progress on their goals – this builds accountability into the conversation and will let you know if more support is needed.

A big part of being a leader is creating an environment that facilitates the development of those around us. When a leader coaches their staff, they act as a catalyst for positive change by helping others find better ways of working together. This creates positive momentum and energy and builds stronger contributions to the important work of our organizations.

REFLECTION QUESTIONS

1. What have you learned from people who have been a catalyst to your own development? What might be important for you to remember from your experience as you work to be a catalyst for others?

2. In what ways are you already a catalyst when it comes to developing those you lead? How can you use the five-step coaching framework to build on employee strengths and help them overcome obstacles in their work?

PRACTICAL APPLICATION

Take some time this week to consider an employee who may need additional support. If appropriate, meet with them and use the five-step coaching framework to guide your conversation. Also, be sure to use this coaching framework the next time you are approached by an employee who is looking for help.

ADDITIONAL RESOURCE

Coaching for Performance: The Principles and Practice of Coaching and Leadership by John Whitmore (Quercus, 2017)

23

COMMUNICATE LIKE YOU'RE ALWAYS ON

BY RANDY GRIESER

As a speaker, I give about five presentations to various groups over the course of a month. Recently I was preparing for an event where there would be 500 people in attendance, and even though the presentation was only an hour long and similar to what I'd delivered before, I invested a lot of time and focus to prepare. When it was time to deliver my presentation, I was confident and ready, and I could see the impact of my keynote on those in attendance.

The week after this presentation, ACHIEVE's monthly organization-wide meeting was scheduled. At these meetings, our leadership team regularly tries to present information and insights in an inspiring way, but sometimes our remarks fall flat. Because this meeting is internal and happens regularly, the truth is that I rarely put the same level of energy into preparation that I would for a keynote speech.

Given the impact of my presentation the week before, I decided to try an experiment. Instead of no or minimal preparation, I put more focus toward planning my introductory remarks for the staff meeting – I gave the same amount of time and attention I would for a larger audience. And as you might imagine, the result was similar – my remarks were more inspirational and better received than they previously had been. It was a stark reminder that if our staff are our most important organizational resource, I should give my communication with them as much attention as I would if I were preparing for a keynote presentation for 500 people.

As leaders we regularly communicate with our staff. We write emails and memos, facilitate meetings, and give organizational updates. Our staff look to us for information, guidance, and inspiration. The words we use matter and either have an impact or don't. And when we fail to give attention to our communication, we risk saying the wrong thing at the wrong time, and we risk losing employee engagement.

The benefits of effective communication are that you are better able to inform, guide, assure, and inspire those you are leading – these are all good and necessary outcomes. However, if your staff are not hearing from you, they will make up their own reality about what is happening or what you are thinking – and it won't always be positive. But leaders who communicate effectively will improve employee engagement and, in the end, promote productivity.

A key part of communicating effectively is to simply invest time and energy into preparation – to give our communication efforts the attention they deserve. However, in addition to time and energy, there are some key principles that I've learned are key to communicating as a leader. Giving attention to the following areas will help you communicate your message in the way you intend it to be heard.

Remember That You're Always On

It's important to understand that you are always communicating. Every interaction you have, word you say, or gesture you make is being listened to and watched by staff. So be aware that you are forever in the spotlight and always delivering a message.

Be Yourself

If you are not honest and sincere in your communication, staff will see through it and tune you out. So be sure to drop the "corporate speak" and communicate with your real voice. Staff will respect and be inspired by straightforward communication, but they will be turned off by anything else. If you are just trying to present yourself as something you're not, people can often see through your efforts.

Keep It Simple

Keep your messages short and simple, not long and convoluted. This increases the likelihood that staff will comprehend what you are saying, and if action is required, they will know how to implement what you are asking them to do.

Be Direct

Be transparent in your communication. Sugarcoating or withholding information from staff will leave them apprehensive or suspicious, and they *will* know that you're not being upfront. If you can't share certain information, come right out and say it, because providing only partial answers breeds distrust.

Always Be Listening

Effective communicators are also good listeners. When you listen well, you gain a clear understanding of how people are feeling and what is needed from leadership. In your conversations with others, listen for the meaning of the message itself *and* listen for any emotions behind it. This will help inform what and how to best communicate about a given situation.

Be Inspirational

One of your roles as a leader is to provide inspiration to those around you – especially in times of crisis. That is why it's up to you to rally your team and motivate them to work toward your common purpose. Monitor the mood of your staff so you can look for opportunities to provide inspiration in times when they need it most.

Use Catchphrases

This may seem awkward for some, but short phrases that highlight your message can catch on and easily become adopted as guiding mantras. For example, one phrase that is part of our innovative culture is "What's next?" It speaks to our desire to never be satisfied with the status quo. When catchphrases are adopted by both leaders and staff, they become a part of the everyday vocabulary, which strengthens their message.

Repeat Yourself

Communication is very prone to becoming distorted. Whether your message is delivered by email, in-person, or via a memo, it will rarely be completely received with the intent you gave it. The best counterbalance to this is repeating what you have to say often and using different mediums. This helps to cement your message and clarify any assumptions.

Successful communication with our staff and effective leadership are intricately connected and have a large impact on organizational success. In our roles as leaders, we communicate across many relationships and settings, both externally and internally. However, we tend to give more attention to those external groups than our internal staff. My encouragement to you is to give just as much attention to your internal communications.

REFLECTION QUESTIONS

1. Think of a time in your role as a leader when you did not communicate well. Looking at the list above, what might have been the reason for this?
2. Which of the areas of communication noted above do you already do well? Which do you need to concentrate on so that you communicate more effectively as a leader?

PRACTICAL APPLICATION

The next time you are communicating with your staff at a meeting or organization-wide gathering, prepare with the same level of attention you would if you were presenting a proposal to a client or stakeholder.

ADDITIONAL RESOURCES

Simply Said: Communicating Better at Work and Beyond by Jay Sullivan (Wiley, 2016)

TED Talk: "How to Speak So That People Want to Listen" by Julian Treasure

24

IN SICKNESS
AND IN HEALTH

BY ERIC STUTZMAN

A friend of mine was recently fired because he had to take time off for a medical procedure. He originally thought he would be off for three days, but after the procedure the doctor advised him that he shouldn't work for two weeks. This may sound extreme (and it is), but when he explained his situation to his boss, he was fired. Aside from whether his boss's response was actually legal or not, it was certainly a shortsighted move that resulted in negative consequences for both my friend *and* the employer.

Consider the message this boss sent to the rest of the employees: *If you need time off – if you are affected adversely by life's events – then you are in danger of losing your job.* The boss's response shows they value short-term productivity more than the people that work for them. If your boss was like this, would you feel comfortable telling them the truth about why you need time off?

In order to have healthy and productive workplaces, we can't expect people to perform at high levels when they are experiencing difficult times in their lives. We will all inevitably experience emotional and physical highs and lows in our lives that result in us needing to take time away from our workplaces – sometimes only for a few hours, but occasionally for much longer periods. We need to create workplaces

When an employee tells a manager that they need time off for a life event, our first response should be to focus on what this means for them.

that both allow for these highs and lows and support the person in getting back to the workplace as soon as is reasonably possible.

Recently in our organization, one colleague got married, while another needed to travel for a funeral and wake that lasted several days. Some of us are supporting aging parents, and one person is caring for a terminally ill family member. And some of us are parents, which means we may need to be at home to take care of our children if they get sick.

It's hard when someone needs to leave for personal or medical matters, but we all understand why the time off is necessary. That is why we do what we can to pitch in and cover for each other when someone needs some time away – we all know that we may require the same support in the future. As a leader, I know that things happen throughout our lives that are outside of our control, and I want my staff to feel supported during these times rather than confined by their work environment.

Leadership sets the tone for responding to requests for time away. In our organization, we want our leadership responses to build trust and loyalty, so we intentionally focus on three areas when faced with a request for time off.

Show Understanding

When an employee tells a manager that they need time off for a life event, our first response should be to focus on what this means *for them*. There will be ample time to consider the impact on the workplace later – use the moment to either celebrate or show empathy. This communicates that the person matters more than a temporary inconvenience at work. When people know that they matter and are cared for, it leads to loyalty, trust, and, we believe, a quicker return to work.

Demonstrate Care

When someone is facing a significant challenge or when they celebrate a life event like a marriage or birth, we try to commemorate it. We do this through simple acts like pitching in some money to provide a meal, sending cards and flowers, or celebrating with a staff potluck and gifts. These small acts of recognition come from both the organization itself and from us as individuals – they mean something because they are physical reminders that we care.

SURVEY STATISTICS

Of those who agreed with the statement, "Leaders in my organization demonstrate care for their staff," 73 percent also reported that their organization has a healthy workplace culture, as opposed to 13 percent of those who disagreed with the statement.

Provide Flexibility

We know that people desire and sometimes need flexibility, so we have made it possible to bank extra time for attending to life's smaller events like medical appointments and school programs. We also provide a short- and long-term disability policy so that if someone runs out of leave time, they can access insurance. In some cases, we have even provided work tools such as a laptop so an employee can work remotely when they need to leave town.

When we respond to requests for time off with these elements in mind, we create an atmosphere where people know they are valued. This leads to expressions of gratitude toward the organization rather than resentment. Treating employees as people first creates the conditions for a great place to work.

REFLECTION QUESTIONS

1. What is your experience with being provided or denied time off for personal or medical reasons? What have you learned about the impact of a leader's response based on your own experience?
2. What is your organization's approach to requests for time off for personal or medical reasons? Are they given begrudgingly or with care and generosity? How might that be impacting employees?

PRACTICAL APPLICATION

Take some time this week to meet as a leadership team and discuss your approach to personal and medical leaves. Talk about the tone of your first responses to employees' requests – are some of you an "easy ask" compared to others? Spend time looking at your leave policies and make any changes that may be needed. Then plan to communicate those changes to staff.

ADDITIONAL RESOURCE

Everybody Matters: The Extraordinary Power of Caring for Your People Like Family by Bob Chapman and Raj Sisodia (Portfolio, 2015)

25
MOVE BEYOND GENDER EQUALITY

BY WENDY LOEWEN

My sister-in-law recently told me a story from when she was a teenager. As she was backing the family car out of the garage, she hit a tree that was planted on the side of the driveway and dented the car. Her mother was home at the time and told her she needed to tell her dad what happened when he came home from work. Needless to say, she was not looking forward to the conversation. Her dad was a hardworking farmer – a serious man of few words. She anticipated an unsympathetic reaction, but her father's response surprised her. All he said was, "That was a bad place to have planted a tree." Her three brothers thought she got off easy. They knew that if it had been one of the boys who had dented the car, his response would have been much stronger.

This story is a funny bit of family history, but it also illustrates the biases some people have when it comes to the expectations around gender. My sister-in-law's treatment revealed that she was not expected to live up to the same driving expectations as her brothers. This incident happened 45 years ago, but biased expectations based on gender are still prevalent. And they go beyond driving – sadly, such biases are still prevalent in many workplaces.

According to data gathered by the *World Economic Forum*, it will take 108 years to close the overall gender gap and 202 years to bring about equity in the workplace.[1] That means we are not likely to reach gender equity in my lifetime or that of my daughter's. Even my grandchildren or great-grandchildren will probably feel the effects of gender inequity in the workplace.

As we explore the current state of gender in the workplace, it is important to make the distinction between gender equality and gender equity. *Gender equality* is about providing the same rights, opportunities, and benefits to everyone regardless of gender, whereas *gender equity* goes a step further to provide supports for those who may struggle to reach the same outcomes as other people. For example, gender equality would mean interviewing both men and women for a position, while gender equity would also mean that the hiring committee works to redress the gender imbalance by making an effort to advertise the position to women and encouraging women to apply. Gender equity recognizes that even if we give people equal access, there will still be barriers to being treated equally – these are the unseen biases and aspects of our systems that perpetuate the status quo of inequality. Promoting gender equity means looking deeply at these barriers and removing them.

If we believe that gender equity – not just equality – matters in our workplaces, then knowing how far we have to go is both disturbing and problematic. Most importantly, this knowledge should propel us to action. At ACHIEVE we are committed to creating more equitable workplaces. As part of our efforts, we recently conducted a survey to find out the experiences of women in leadership and in the workplace. The survey data reiterated the prevalence of differing expectations based on gender, much like what my sister-in-law experienced 45 years ago.

The findings verified that although there have been advances in gender equality, it is clear that we still have a long way to go. For example, one interesting finding from our survey was about attractiveness and how it supports advancement in leadership. Attractiveness was mainly seen as helpful for women. Only 27 percent agreed or strongly agreed that attractiveness helps advance men in leadership positions,

Promoting gender equity means looking deeply at these barriers and removing them.

while 41 percent agreed or strongly agreed that attractiveness helps women.[2]

Gender inequity continues because many of our workplace systems are set up in such a way that they perpetuate gender inequity. A study by *Harvard Business Review* states that if there is one woman in a candidate pool of four people, statistically there is a zero percent chance (yes, zero percent, sadly that is not a typo) that she will get the position.[3] A single woman among a group of men stands out as different, and human beings like to perpetuate the status quo. The article goes on to point out that 95 percent of CEOs are men and less than 35 percent of managers are women, and that this statistic isn't likely to change without intervention.[4]

So, what can we do to help the move toward equity? I don't think there are easy answers to this question, but I do know that the first step to solving any problem is moving from awareness to action. A good place to start is by critically assessing your workplace. I appreciate that this can feel like a daunting task, but from my experience both as an employee and now as a leader within an organization striving for gender equity, there are five key things organizations can do to start building a more equitable workplace.

Establish Clear Goals

Complete a review of your workplace and make a plan to improve gender diversity. Ask your employees about areas where they see possibility for improvement and use the information to establish goals to really move the needle. Be sure to communicate these to your staff and keep yourself accountable to meeting these goals.

Evaluate Your Hiring Practices

Review your job advertisements and interview questions to ensure they are gender neutral. Use descriptive words that apply to the whole gender spectrum. Make sure that all job titles are gender neutral, for example, salesperson rather than salesman. Provide bias-awareness training to all involved in the hiring process. Also, ensure you have women on your hiring committees and allow them to give input when making hiring decisions.

Examine Your Pay Structure

Conduct a pay audit. Be on the lookout for discrepancies between the rate of pay among staff who have similar experience and comparable roles. If you note inconsistencies, make a commitment to equalizing the pay structure.

Reevaluate Your Promotion Process

Equity in the workplace is not simply about having equal numerical representation of all genders in your organization (although this is a good place to start). It is also about who holds what position – especially when it comes to leadership roles. Equity is about the *quality* of employment that is available and how transitions are created, planned for, and shared among genders. Capacity building and opportunities for training and advancement should not be dependent on gender.

Gender equity contributes to a vital workplace culture. In our survey on women in leadership, 68 percent of those who agreed that their workplaces were committed to equal gender representation in leadership also said they had a healthy workplace culture; only 18 percent of those who disagreed that their workplaces were committed to equal gender representation in leadership also said they have a strong workplace culture.[5] It's clear from the survey that workplaces that are committed to equal gender representation tend to have happy, satisfied employees and teams that work well together. Although we did not assess equity in our study, we did see a positive impact on workplace culture when there is equal gender representation. We believe that a commitment to equal gender representation is predicated on creating equity.

Gender inequity means certain voices are underrepresented in the workplace and, in some cases, they are not represented at all. This means we miss out on ideas, creativity, and influence simply because we do not have gender equity, and our overall culture suffers. It is time we consider the implications of gender inequity and work to make the future different. The sooner we begin, the better.

REFLECTION QUESTIONS

1. How is your organization ensuring that it promotes and maintains gender equality? How close are you to achieving gender equality?
2. What is one tangible thing you can do to make a positive impact that will move your organization toward greater gender equity?

PRACTICAL APPLICATION

Within the next month, meet with your leadership team to consider the health of your workplace culture as it relates to gender equity. Look at each department and the gender makeup of the various levels of management to determine where your organization is in terms of gender representation. Ask women, in safe ways, about their experience with equity in your organization. Look for ways to work toward gender equity for *all*. What would need to change on a policy level or on a practical level?

ADDITIONAL RESOURCE

The Moment of Lift: How Empowering Women Changes the World by Melinda Gates (Flatiron Books, 2019)

26

LEAD WITH A
SENSE OF URGENCY

BY RANDY GRIESER

I have always lived my life with a certain level of urgency. All through my school years, I regularly completed my assignments well in advance. As a teenager, I was antsy to leave home to attend university, and by my second year I was ready to graduate and get my first "real" job. Once I started working, it wasn't long before I needed something more. This led to the creation of ACHIEVE Centre for Leadership.

For over 15 years, I have been leading our organization through both challenges and opportunities, and I firmly believe that leading with a sense of urgency has been key to our success. I have always encouraged our staff to push harder and faster when it comes to implementing new changes or navigating difficulties. However, they must also balance the urgency with *thoughtful intention* – thinking before acting and slowing down just enough to consider all the factors before proceeding. Over time this way of operating has become embedded in our culture and is now "the way we do things around here." This approach has served us well, both in normal times and when managing critical moments.

The most recent crisis we've had to navigate is the COVID-19 pandemic. Like many organizations, at the start of the pandemic we were in a critical state. We had a significant decrease in income, which required us to make major decisions around expenses and personnel in order to stay viable. Because we are a training organization in the business of bringing people together – mostly in person – getting back to our "normal" wasn't going to happen anytime soon.

This new reality was a challenge, but, given our history of leading with a sense of urgency, our team was ready and willing to meet it. Over the course of a week, we pivoted from an organization that offers in-person training to one that offers online training. And over the following months, we fine-tuned our processes, and the result was better than anyone could have imagined. We focused our attention on creating highly engaging and accessible online training opportunities – and our clients responded positively.

I believe our ability to pivot so quickly was possible because this was not the first time we had adjusted our ways of operating or needed to quickly implement changes. In fact, leading with a sense of urgency has never solely been about managing crises – it's the way we function in *both* good times and bad times.

SURVEY QUOTE

An effective leader can pivot and understands that things do not always run smoothly despite diligent planning and preparation.

The need to lead with a sense urgency during a crisis is not foreign to most leaders, but too many reserve this style of leadership for emergencies. I believe organizations function better when leaders also lead with a sense of urgency in good times. The same focused energy required to navigate a crisis can net great benefits when it's used to search for opportunities and attend to day-to-day operational matters. Practically, this means being innovative and productive. It means implementing a different idea or starting a new project *now* – and making sure it's finished on time. It means striving for great rather than settling for good. Leading this way in times when people aren't in a heightened emotional state is good practice for when a crisis does occur. It's important to be intentional about *how* to lead with urgency, and this is best learned in situations that aren't so intense.

When organizations and leaders who are not used to leading with urgency are forced to because of a crisis, they often focus their energy in the wrong way. Making a quick plan or deciding on an action does *not* mean it's the right thing to do. That is why it's important to consider if you are leading with the right kind of urgency – are you leading with focused urgency or unfocused urgency?

Unfocused urgency is normally born out of excessive fear and anxiety and tends to lead to bad decisions, increased mistakes, and stress for staff and leaders. Although this type of urgency does create activity and movement, it often doesn't lead to the kind of productivity or innovation that moves the organization forward. With unfocused urgency there is too much focus on *doing something*, and often it's not the "right" something.

The act of doing something often leads to a false sense of accomplishment and security. In fact, organizations may decide not to continue to look for ways of navigating the situation because something has already been done. However, doing the "wrong" something is usually worse than doing nothing at all.

Acting out of panic and fear is not the same as *focused urgency*, which is rooted in approaching the issue with thoughtful intention. While focused urgency still creates the desire to do things *now* – not *someday* – it also allows time for us to slow down long enough to make sure we aren't overreacting or making a decision or plan that will have a negative ripple effect a month or even years down the line. We have found two practical ways to practice focused urgency.

Proactively Deal With Challenges

When challenges arise, avoid incorporating a wait-and-see approach. You don't need to implement every idea for how to approach the challenge, but you do need to start developing a plan with your team right away – and you need to do so calmly. Be sure to have discussions and generate ideas from all levels of the organization, not just at the leadership level.

Look For and Seize Opportunities Right Away

Organizations will have a hard time seizing opportunities if they aren't looking for them. In his book, *A Sense of Urgency*, John Kotter notes, "External change must be seen to be acted upon. With an insufficient sense of urgency, people don't tend to look hard enough or can't seem to find the time to look hard enough."[1] In addition to leadership watching for opportunities, staff should be encouraged to be on the lookout as well. When a decision is made to pursue an opportunity, start it right away, and make sure staff have the resources needed to pursue it.

To effectively harness the power of focused urgency, we need to become more intentional and less reactive. This gives us heightened focus and clarity to navigate challenges and be on the lookout for opportunities that will not only help us now, but also in the future.

REFLECTION QUESTIONS

1. What are some examples of leading with *unfocused urgency* you have experienced as a leader? What was the impact of this approach?

2. Think about people you know who lead with *focused urgency* or times when you have led in this way. What have you learned from these experiences that you could bring to your regular leadership practice?

PRACTICAL APPLICATION

Remember, you don't have to wait for a crisis to lead with a sense of urgency – you can start right now. Consider the projects you are currently working on or decisions you need to make this week and develop plans to tackle them with focused urgency. In all your projects, work to make leading with a sense of urgency the norm, not the exception.

ADDITIONAL RESOURCE

A Sense of Urgency by John Kotter (Harvard Business Review Press, 2008)

27

ARE YOU CONTROLLING OR CONNECTING?

BY ERIC STUTZMAN

A number of years ago I was a newly minted director in a large national organization. Each year, about 60 leaders within this organization met to do work on governance and policy-related items. At one meeting, our CEO, a physically imposing man with a booming voice and an emotional style of leadership, called on me to share my perspective about a contentious issue. With some nervousness, I expressed my alternate view of the matter being debated. The CEO leaned forward at the table with a look of consternation on his face, threw his hands in the air, and said in his loud voice, "Ah, come on, Eric! You know that isn't true!"

Like most people, I don't normally say things that I believe are untrue. Nor do I like to be shut down by my leader after taking a risk in front of a group at his invitation. The reality is that the impact of that moment was significant for me – I was embarrassed and no longer felt free to talk about what I really thought. Although I was aware that the CEO often reacted in an emotional way, the saving grace in this situation was that I also knew he was a good-hearted person who cared about me. If it had been otherwise, I would have started to look for a new job right away.

Leaders affect their staff in profound ways through their style of leadership, and yet they often do not realize the extent of their impact. This is particularly problematic because the voices of leaders are amplified by their position of power within the hierarchy of an organization. When a leader speaks or acts, it carries more weight due to their position of influence. Their emotions are felt more keenly, and their opinions sway others more strongly than other employees' perspectives.

I believe all leaders need to dedicate time to developing self-awareness about their leadership style in a way that moves beyond strengths and weaknesses. Although these things may affect our leadership style, they are not the same thing. Leadership style is essentially the way other colleagues experience us in the workplace – how others describe our presence and our approach. When we understand our natural leadership style, we can make conscious choices about how to use that style or even shift our approach in a given set of circumstances to get different results. When we develop self-awareness, we can be more intentional about how we want to be experienced.

Although there are many ways to think about or categorize leadership style, I have found that Clifford Nass' distillation of personality in his book, *The Man Who Lied to His Laptop*, creates a simple and powerful way to also think about leadership. He notes that all people are experienced along two continuums: expression of *control* and expression of interpersonal *connection*.[1] Each continuum has a low end and a high end.

Leaders Are Experienced on Two Continuums

Control/Influence
LOW   HIGH

Connection
LOW   HIGH

Leaders affect their staff in profound ways through their style of leadership, and yet they often do not realize the extent of their impact.

I have found it is helpful to think about these continuums in the context of leadership. Along the *control* continuum, staff may experience their leaders as exerting very little control to very high control when it comes to their work and the decisions that affect them. This continuum is about how leaders wield their influence and apply their ideas to the day-to-day work of staff. To place yourself on this continuum, consider whether you are experienced as rarely giving input or controlling your team's work, giving lots of input and making decisions for staff, or somewhere in between. Someone at the low end of this spectrum will appear absent from day-to-day decision-making and will rarely express their opinion about the details of their employees' work. By contrast, someone at the highest end of this spectrum will be involved in many details of the daily work and will regularly assert themselves when it comes to decisions.

The *connection* continuum refers to the degree to which leaders relate to staff on a personal level. One way to understand this continuum is to think about it in terms of relational coolness or warmth. To place yourself on the continuum, consider whether you are experienced as cool and disconnected, warm and highly connected, or somewhere in the middle. Someone at the low end of this spectrum will seem disconnected from the daily conversations and relationships in the organization. They may be thought of as cold or uninterested in their colleagues. At the highest end of this spectrum, the leader is connected to the personal lives of their staff and is seen as warm and highly relational.

When taken together, these two continuums create four broad leadership styles:

- **The Absent Leader:** This is a leader who is experienced as low on control and low on connection.
- **The Cheerleader:** This is a leader who is experienced as low on control but high on connection.
- **The Authoritarian Leader:** This is a leader who is experienced as high on control but low on connection.
- **The Collaborative Leader:** This is the leader who is experienced as high on both control and connection.

Four Styles of Leadership

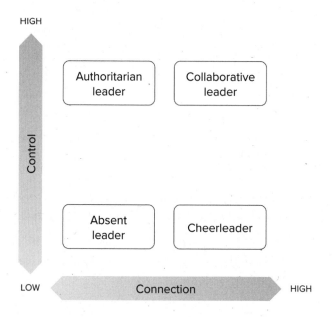

Given the complexity of our organizations and teams, different leadership styles may be called for at different times. In a time of crisis, a leader may need to act with authority, exert control, and not worry about relationships in the moment (e.g., "There's a fire! Everybody get out! No, we are not going to make sure everyone feels okay about this first."). A team of experienced staff who understand their work may require a leader to cheer them on much of the time. And in many situations, it is important for a leader to assert their ideas in the context of warm and collaborative relationships.

While different situations may call for different leadership styles, leaders need to be aware of the potential downside of an approach. For instance, an authoritarian style may create compliance, but it rarely promotes critical thinking, ownership, and creativity. A leader who cheers staff on will help people feel good but may struggle to hold them accountable. An absent leader will give the impression that they don't care about the team or their work, resulting in an atmosphere of ambiguity. While a collaborative approach is useful in most instances, it can be less effective for dealing with emergencies and can lead to collaboration fatigue if overused.

Most leaders tend to express one style more strongly than others. However, I have often witnessed leaders, myself included, shifting their style when facing stress or when they are acting unconsciously. The most effective leaders know their tendencies regarding control and connection and then work to make conscious decisions about how they want to be experienced. For instance, I have learned that as I get busier or more stressed, I am likely to spend less time on connection and am more likely to assert myself – this results in my team experiencing me as more authoritarian. Since I believe that collaborative leadership is the most effective leadership style in most instances, I need to counteract my natural tendencies in times of stress by consciously adding connection.

In modern workplaces many people will prefer that their leaders express a collaborative style of leadership most of the time. I believe this is as it should be. For most jobs, people are hired to use their brains. This requires leaders to build strong relationships that make it safe for people to contribute. It also requires leaders to enter conversations with self-awareness and contribute their own ideas in ways that do not overpower the ideas of others.

We all need to develop self-awareness so that we can express a leadership style that is appropriate for our circumstances and our team.

Through developing awareness about our tendencies regarding control and connection, we can decide whether we want to do what comes naturally or what is best for our team. And remember that, in most cases, our teams will expect or at least hope for us to be collaborative leaders.

REFLECTION QUESTIONS

1. How do you think you are experienced by those you lead when it comes to the continuums of connection and control? What happens to your leadership style as you face different situations or increasing stress? Do you change styles?
2. How could you become more conscious about your leadership style and the impact it may have on staff? What about other leaders in your organization – how conscious are they and what could be done to raise the collective consciousness level of the leadership team?

PRACTICAL APPLICATION

In the next week, block out some time for developing your self-awareness. Think about how much time you invest in relationships and in showing warmth to others. Also consider how often you exert your influence into the work and decisions of your staff. Ask someone you trust to give you their assessment of how you are experienced when it comes to connection and control and see if that lines up with your own assessment.

ADDITIONAL RESOURCE

The Man Who Lied to His Laptop: What We Can Learn About Ourselves from Our Machines by Clifford Nass and Corina Yen (Current, 2012)

28
ALWAYS TELL
THE TRUTH

BY WENDY LOEWEN

When I was 16, my parents bought a Volkswagen Beetle that we, like so many others, named "The Bug." My parents appreciated the fuel efficiency, and I loved that it was a "cool car." A few years later, my family bought another Volkswagen, a yellow Rabbit. My parents liked the fuel efficiency, and I loved the color. Our next car was yet another Volkswagen, this time a white diesel Jetta. Although I would have preferred something flashier than plain white, again my parents chose it for the fuel efficiency.

These three family cars immediately came to mind in 2015 when the news hit that Volkswagen had lied about fuel economy and cheated on its emissions tests for a whopping 11 million cars sold over seven years.[1] When I heard this, I felt angry and deceived. As the story unfolded, it became clear that the leadership at Volkswagen were aware of the issues with their cars. However, rather than responding with integrity, leadership decided not to correct the problem. Apparently, the financial rewards of cheating on the tests and potential cost of addressing the issues were too great. Their actions are a sad example of leaders behaving with a lack of integrity.

Ironically, in 2011 Volkswagen publicly stated that "By working in co-operation with politicians and society, the world of business can play a key part when it comes to combating serious environmental issues and social inequality."[2] The 2015 scandal, since named Dieselgate, raised awareness of the pollution levels emitted by diesel vehicles – and it also highlighted the importance of leading with integrity. When Volkswagen was caught, their leadership did publicly apologize. "We've totally screwed up," they said in one statement; and in another, "We have broken the trust of our customers and the public."[3] But acting with integrity means taking responsibility for our actions when we realize the negative impact of our behavior because it is the right thing to do, not because we were caught. If Volkswagen actually cared about their emissions, they would have changed their practices *before* being called out.

In all organizations, a lack of integrity not only affects overall reputation, but it also has a direct impact on staff. In a recent conversation with a colleague, she shared that one of the reasons she trusts the leaders at ACHIEVE is that they act with integrity. She is not alone – in a study on the topic, *Forbes* cited integrity as *the most important* leadership attribute, reporting that 75 percent of the employees surveyed named integrity as the most vital characteristic for a leader.[4]

SURVEY QUOTE

Integrity is huge. An honest and trustworthy leader will help inspire the followers. If employees know they can trust their leader, the whole workplace can work together more effectively.

Employees want their leaders to have good moral character and be consistently trustworthy. It is often easy to say the right words – as was the case with Volkswagen – but integrity needs to be visible in both words *and* actions. How do we as leaders live out and demonstrate integrity?

Over the years I have come to see that integrity is demonstrated in three main ways. First and foremost, we as leaders need to follow the laws of our country and not engage in illegal actions – this should go without saying, but it warrants a strong reminder. Do a quick search and you will see a host of examples of leaders breaking the law. A study by *Harvard Business Review* found that employers sometimes push their staff to engage in illegal actions, and some even directly ask them to act unethically on behalf of the organization.[5] These kinds of unethical actions alienate staff and create a culture where dishonesty is perpetuated. They also tarnish the public reputation of an organization when such behavior comes to light.

Second, acting with integrity means following your organization's internal policies and organizational values. In my consulting work, I have heard many people say that their managers and supervisors do not abide by the same expectations and guidelines they are expected to follow. These are smaller infractions than breaking the law, but the effect is nonetheless detrimental. This type of action communicates that workplace rules don't apply to everyone. Staff become cynical as leaders talk the talk but don't walk the walk. In our organization we have a workplace policy outlining that we expect people to speak respectfully to each other. We hold our staff to this and keep leadership accountable to do the same. "Flexibility" is also one of our core values, meaning we expect our staff to pitch in as needed, even when it falls outside the scope of their regular duties. Leading with integrity means that our staff can count on and expect the same from us.

Lastly, acting with integrity calls us to a higher standard than just the letter of the law or our internal policies and organizational values. Acting with integrity is demonstrated when we act within the spirit and intention of the laws, codes, and treaties around us; in other words, leading with a strong moral compass. As leaders, we should be able to identify our personal values and act in accordance with them. Telling the truth and treating people with respect should matter to us because they are the right ways to behave, not because they are contained in our organization's list of values. We should constantly be asking ourselves, "What are my values?" "How do I express them in my day-to-day actions?" "What are my moral obligations?" and "How do I demonstrate my integrity beyond just following the rules?"

I recently asked one of my staff what integrity in leadership meant for her. After thinking for a moment, she said that she knows that she can count on leadership to do what they say they will, and that what they say is true and honest – even when it's difficult. In my work I often hear leaders wrestle with how to build trust, but one of the simplest ways is to lead with integrity. Our staff, clients, and even the general public expect leaders to act with integrity – and when we do, we gain their trust. And if they trust our direction, then they can feel secure with our guidance, even when they don't have all the information.

Leaders set the tone for the larger organization, which is why we have an obligation and responsibility to act in ways that promote honesty and integrity. It is not good enough to just know the right words to say; our actions need to match our words or else they ring hollow. Regardless of how charismatic or visionary we are, our integrity will affect the impact we can have on others. As we strive to lead with integrity, we can't become complacent – we need to keep assessing where we are at, knowing that when we lead with integrity, we have the potential to create a better workplace and perhaps a better world.

REFLECTION QUESTIONS

1. What are your memories or experiences of leaders acting without integrity? What impact did these experiences have on you?
2. What does "leading with integrity" mean to you? Who will hold you accountable to acting with integrity in your role as a leader?

PRACTICAL APPLICATION

Think about situations in your organization where you have seen people act with honesty and integrity, even when it was difficult. Then consider the areas in which it may be difficult. Discuss these with your leadership team and plan out how you act with integrity. In your conversations consider the three areas above: behaving ethically and legally, following your organization's policies and values, and acting on your own moral compass.

ADDITIONAL RESOURCE

The Character Edge: Leading and Winning with Integrity by Robert L. Caslen, Jr. and Michael D. Matthews (St. Martin's Press, 2021)

29

TRAUMA-INFORMED LEADERSHIP

BY RANDY GRIESER

Given my clinical training as a social worker and my past experiences of working with trauma in a variety of settings, I have some unique perspectives about how trauma impacts the workplace. After transitioning out of direct social work practice, one of the things I quickly realized was that trauma's effects are not limited to healthcare or social service settings. Trauma has a tendency to seep into workplaces and impact people's behavior, performance, and relationships. That is why it's crucial for all leaders to strive to create trauma-informed workplaces.

Trauma occurs when a person or group is confronted with a threat to themselves or others and that threat overwhelms their coping resources and affects their physical, mental, emotional, relational, and spiritual health. Trauma is prevalent in our world and impacts all of us, including our staff, colleagues, and clients. The effects of trauma can ripple across all areas of a person's life and shape their interactions and relationships at home and at work. It even affects whole organizations by impacting the ways in which we do our work, serve our clients, and achieve our missions.

Our workplaces can be negatively influenced by the pervasive power of trauma, and they can also unintentionally amplify its impacts.

However, by embracing trauma-informed principles, our organizations can also contribute to the positive transformation of individuals and relationships affected by trauma.

Trauma-informed workplaces understand the presence of trauma, acknowledge the role trauma can play in a person's life, and promote work environments that support the individual and collective well-being of all staff and clients.* They create a sense of belonging, connection, and safety through their attitudes, policies, and practices. As a result, organizations that are trauma-informed are more resilient and better able to achieve their missions. *Every* workplace, in *every* sector, can benefit from becoming trauma-informed.

In *A Little Book About Trauma-Informed Workplaces*, my co-authors and I outline five key principles that trauma-informed organizations embody. These principles are described below.

Promote Awareness

In trauma-informed organizations, leaders and employees are aware of the pervasiveness of trauma and its significance in people's lives. They understand that when anyone's sense of well-being or survival is threatened, it can cause lasting emotional and psychological injury. They know that the subsequent effects will usually cause vulnerability and influence how staff and clients engage with supports, handle stress, perform their tasks, and simply maintain hope and energy to function.

Educating staff about trauma is integral to generating awareness. All those who work in the organization should be provided with opportunities to grow in their awareness of the prevalence and impacts of trauma and apply this learning to their work. Regardless of the specific route taken to promote awareness, training should encourage thoughtful reflection about trauma and explore how to create mean-

---

* A note about language: while the following information is for all types of workplaces, going forward the term "client" is used, which could also refer to a student, customer, or any other recipient of your services.

ingful interactions. This is optimally done through relationships and connection with others.

Shift Attitudes

While trauma awareness is valuable at a *knowledge* level, an *attitude* shift is necessary in order to change how we engage with people. By shifting attitudes, we are able to *put our awareness of trauma into action*. This shift impacts the questions we ask and creates a mindset of curious empathy that we can bring to our interactions. It is demonstrated by responding to people, organizations, and communities in ways that reflect awareness of the role trauma can have. When we shift our attitudes, our biases recede and healthy responses to trauma become the norm.

Traumatic experiences can cause people to react with the protective survival instincts of fight, flight, and freeze behaviors. Because these survival instincts can also emerge in everyday situations that aren't actually threatening, these behaviors are often misunderstood and difficult to respond to. While they are useful in the face of actual threats, they can come across as unhelpful or challenging when they don't seem to match the situation. When we recognize the possibility that trauma may be a factor in these behaviors, we can understand and approach them with an attitude of empathetic curiosity.

Foster Safety

One of the central aspects of trauma is the experience of a threat to physical or psychological safety. This threat can continue to affect a person's ability to feel fully safe in future environments and situations. When an organization does not give attention to safety, it can make both staff and clients vulnerable and create barriers to engagement. Therefore, fostering safety helps reduce the impact of past damaging experiences.

Fostering a safe environment requires paying close attention to the varying needs of different people. These can range from the physical, such as the need for adequate lighting and safety rails, to the psychological, which could include managing conflict or disrespectful behavior. It is important to consider both the physical *and* psychological elements of safety. Too often, those responsible for safety limit their focus to physical areas or only give token attention to psychological concerns.

Provide Choice

A significant aspect of traumatic events is the lack of choice and control that people experience. The helplessness felt in an overwhelmingly threatening situation can leave lasting imprints on a person's sense of power to take back control over their lives. Therefore, it's important for trauma-informed workplaces to provide *meaningful* opportunities for choice.

Offering opportunities for choice can be a juggling act of consulting, reconciling differences, and sharing responsibility. Providing staff and clients with choices means respecting their unique identities and affirming the natural diversity among individuals and communities. It means intentionally inviting minority voices and those with less organizational power to share their experiences and suggestions. At times, it will require us to respect the choices and voices that run contrary to – or even challenge – the status quo. These challenging voices are to be expected, and it is through these conversations that we can begin to create healthier, more trauma-informed workplaces.

Highlight Strengths

Every person has inherent strengths that help them survive. For people who have come through traumatic experiences, highlighting strengths is especially relevant because it helps to emphasize and build up their inherent resilience. After all, they have survived *because of their strengths* and have found new and creative ways to live and overcome obstacles.

Unfortunately, rather than focusing on strengths, organizations sometimes emphasize the differences, problems, and weaknesses of staff and clients. This can lead to withdrawal, low morale, disconnection, and, at worst, re-traumatization. However, when we identify what is going well and build on these successes, the powers of resilience and connection can take hold and flourish. Resilience is the ability to survive and adapt in the face of stress and adverse life experiences, and it is extremely valuable for healing from trauma.

Becoming trauma-informed is not a simple, straightforward process – it may take an organization in multiple directions instead of on a linear path. It takes hard work, and there may be successes in one area followed by setbacks in another. Just as the impacts of trauma are complex, the implementation of trauma-informed principles can be complicated. But by working intentionally, following the principles, and asking thoughtful questions, leaders can help their organizations navigate the process with care and consideration.

REFLECTION QUESTIONS

1. How have you seen the ripple effects of trauma impact your organization?
2. What specific steps could your organization take to become more trauma-informed?

PRACTICAL APPLICATION

Start with building your organization's awareness of trauma. Arrange an in-person training day for your staff, access online training, or read the book listed below together. Whatever form of training you choose, be sure to spend time discussing the insights learned. To help you assess and understand the level of your organization's trauma-informed awareness and practice, you can also access our free Trauma-Informed Workplace Assessment by visiting the Free Resources section of the Crisis & Trauma Resource Institute's website at www.ctrinstitute.com.

ADDITIONAL RESOURCE

A Little Book About Trauma-Informed Workplaces by Nathan Gerbrandt, Randy Grieser, and Vicki Enns (ACHIEVE Publishing, 2021)

30
IS YOUR
FEEDBACK FAIR?

BY ERIC STUTZMAN

We all need feedback in order to grow. It helps us learn how our actions impact other people and whether we have been effective in what we are doing. Despite our need for feedback, the word often carries a negative association. This is because when it is given in unhelpful ways, it often does more harm than good. Many of us even fear feedback because it has been delivered to us so poorly in the past.

A friend of mine was recently caught off guard and hurt when his manager handed him a letter at 4:22 p.m. on a Friday. The letter outlined a series of complaints, some of which he didn't even remember. He asked if he could discuss the letter, but the manager responded with "No, we'll talk about it on Monday."

In my view, this is a very unfair approach to feedback – and it's ineffective. Let's imagine that the manager did have something that was important for my friend to hear. By delivering the feedback right before the weekend and shutting down the opportunity for dialogue, any chance for it to be well-received was eliminated. Instead, my friend was left to stew with his unanswered questions all weekend long. It did not enhance his desire to enthusiastically engage in a conversation about ways he could improve when he came back on Monday.

There are many things leaders can do to strengthen the effectiveness of their feedback. Here are eight principles for giving feedback in a way that is fair and maximizes the chances for it to be well received.

Remember That Feedback Is about Learning

Begin by remembering that feedback is about learning and improvement. As with all teaching or coaching, keep the desired outcome at the center so that you remain focused. It is ineffective if feedback is delivered in such a way that the recipient cannot internalize and act on it to reach the desired outcome. The question we should ask is, "What conditions and approach to feedback will lead to the desired outcome?" One of the most powerful ways to promote learning is to affirm what someone has done well. When you notice what someone has done right, they are more likely to repeat and build on that behavior.

Start with a Question

It is too easy to misunderstand what we see or experience from another person. Before launching into your feedback, take a moment to pause and get curious about what you have seen. Then name the action or behavior and ask the other person for their perspective on what they did. As you listen to their response, consider whether there is a disconnect between what they say their intention was and the impact of their actions. If you have misunderstood the situation, you may be able to let your feedback go at this point. However, if they need to understand the impact of their actions, then proceed with your feedback.

Provide Feedback Immediately

It's easy for managers to let small things slide and store them up for a larger conversation. However, if you bring up multiple issues at once, you run the risk of overwhelming the employee. Most people learn best when their mistakes are pointed out to them soon after they happen. This allows them to reflect on the issue while it's still fresh in their memory. It also prevents them from forming a habit based on an incorrect way of doing things. Instead of making a list of things someone has done wrong and then giving it to them in a meeting, talk to them about issues as they arise.

Be Mindful of *When* You Give Feedback

When it's not possible to give feedback in the moment, consider other times when the employee will be receptive to what you have to say. Avoid giving feedback right before the person has to attend a meeting, office party, or give a presentation – and don't discuss the issue right before they have days off. People often ruminate on feedback, and it is not fair to the employee to have them do so on their time off. In addition to this, I think people need to consider the feedback they receive while they are in the midst of their work so they can immediately apply what they have heard to real situations. This helps with integrating the new information. If you are planning to give feedback, try meeting earlier in the employee's work week so they can immediately consider and implement what they have heard.

Be Mindful of *Where* You Give Feedback

Depending on what the feedback is about, consider whether it should be given privately. If your feedback is related to a specific behavior, you risk embarrassing the receiver if it's given in front of others. This will make it much harder for them to accept what you have to say. Although your feedback might not seem like a big issue to you, it may be significant for the employee. Some people will want privacy so that they can process what you are saying without distraction, even if it is mild or positive.

Focus On Behavior, Not Character

One of the most common mistakes that managers make when giving feedback is making assumptions about the employee's character. For instance, you might think an employee has been coming late to meetings because they don't care, or that someone didn't volunteer for an assignment because they are trying to get away with only doing the bare minimum. Speculating in this way ultimately clouds your ability to give feedback about specific behaviors. It can cause you to focus on something you don't like about the person, or treat a person differently based on a false assumption.

If you want to be an effective manager, concentrate on a specific behavior that needs to change. Focusing on character creates defensiveness; focusing on behavior and its impact creates an opportunity for learning.

Make the Conversation about Their Interests, Too

As a manager, you should always try to include the employee's interests in the feedback conversation in addition to yours. That means focusing on why you want to have the conversation from a management perspective *and* why this might be valuable for the employee's own interests. Practically speaking, your interest in giving feedback is normally to help the employee do their job better. An employee's interests will often include being seen as competent, valuable, and doing their job well.

To bring the employee's interests into the conversation, express your positive intention in giving them feedback. Explain how you are confident that they want to do their job as well as possible and that you believe they would want to know if they were doing something that could be preventing them from performing at their best.

Discuss a Positive Vision for the Future

Your conversation should finish with a plan so that the employee knows what their next steps should be. Talk with the employee about what they can do differently based on your feedback. Make sure the conversation is specific and framed in the language of behavior, not character.

Remember to also build in a plan for assessing how the changes are going. This can be as simple as planning a follow-up meeting to check in. Let them know you are there to support them as they integrate the feedback and make any necessary changes. You might even want to provide training or other supports. Thank them for taking the time to have the conversation with you.

Everyone needs feedback to improve – and everyone deserves to be treated with respect when receiving it. Feedback should be a conversation that protects the dignity of the employee, upholds your professional integrity, and clearly communicates what changes need to be made. Following the principles outlined above will help you deliver feedback that is fair and well received.

REFLECTION QUESTIONS

1. When have you received feedback in a way that made it easier to accept, learn from, and implement the changes? What made that possible for you?
2. Consider how you and other leaders in your organization currently provide feedback. Using the principles above, what practical steps can you take to improve your delivery so that feedback has a better chance of being received well?

PRACTICAL APPLICATION

The next time you need to give someone feedback, review the principles above and discuss your planned conversation with a peer. Have them give *you* feedback on what might improve the clarity of what you're trying to say and to ensure the feedback is reasonable. This will help you approach the feedback conversation with more confidence and clarity.

ADDITIONAL RESOURCE

Nonviolent Communication: A Language of Life by Marshall Rosenberg (PuddleDancer Press, 2015)

31
GROW STRONGER TOGETHER

BY WENDY LOEWEN

When I was young, I showed horses. During competitions, the judge would stand in the center of the arena to adjudicate our performance. At the end of the competition, riders would line up side-by-side in front of the judge to find out how they did. As the judge announced the winners, the audience would cheer, and the winner would ride forward to receive their award. Sometimes the judges would even provide feedback on what the winners had done well and where the rest of us had fallen short. For many years, my name was never called, and I would leave without a ribbon for my hard work.

After telling this story recently, someone asked me about how the experience of *not* winning affected my self-esteem. They assumed that it was demotivating, but in reality it had the opposite effect. I did not spend long hours grooming my horse, cleaning the stalls, and practicing my riding skills simply to beat others – I was showing horses because I wanted to get better at it and spend time around others who were *already* better than me so I could learn from them and improve. It took some years, but I did collect a few trophies and ribbons. The award I am most proud of is a silver platter – it now has a few rust stains, but you can still read the writing: "Most Improved."

Sitting in the middle of the arena with all those skilled riders made me feel like I was in the winner's circle, and it was inspiring. Being part of a group where everyone was committed to excellence was energizing. I could ask them questions, watch them in action, and try to mirror what they did. They were examples of what I aspired to be. They accepted and encouraged me to keep striving to get better. I came to see that if I worked hard, someday I could be as good as they were. And when the judge outlined what the winners did well, I listened intently. When they pointed out areas of improvement, I paid attention and went home to practice. It was an environment that provided all the opportunities I needed to develop my skills.

Although there are a few things I got wrong in my teenage years, my attitude toward development was one thing that I got right – and it is something I have also brought to my role as a leader. In our workplaces, the best leaders work to provide environments where employees are inspired to continually develop and grow. This happens when we are surrounded by excellence in a workplace where we recognize who is good at what and encourage others to learn from the examples around them. Following are a few ideas to help you create a culture where team members share a passion for continuous improvement.

Encourage People to Work Together

Many organizations have a culture that is so focused on individual performance and accountability that they forego the opportunity to capitalize on the positive influence of a group in promoting development. My grandpa used to say, "Iron sharpens iron," and when I asked him what this meant, he explained that when the iron blades of two knives are rubbed together, they become sharper and more effective as a result. He said that the same effect happens when we surround

The best leaders work to provide environments where employees are inspired to continually develop and grow.

ourselves with good people – they influence us, and we tend to emulate their positive characteristics.

This idea holds true in the workplace. When we encourage our staff to work together on projects, they will naturally learn from one another as they interact, ask questions, and experience the combined energy of their skills.

Provide Opportunities to Learn about Each Other's Roles

There is real value in having our employees be aware of what happens in the various departments in our organization. We don't need to plunge our staff into unrelated roles for the purpose of simply learning what their coworkers do, but we do want them to understand how their role contributes to the organization's mission.

One way that we have done this at ACHIEVE is to have new hires sit for 15–20 minutes with each employee during their first week on the job. This gives them the opportunity to see the expertise of other staff and builds a sense of pride as employees highlight their unique contributions. It also provides staff with the knowledge of who they can go to when they need help or who they could approach if they want to develop their own skills in a particular area. In addition, when we highlight that they are surrounded by people who excel at what they do, it encourages them to become exceptional in their role.

Facilitate Peer-to-Peer Training

Some of the managers I have spoken with have the perception that the "experts" are outside their organization. Although this may be true in some cases, this mindset can result in the skills of their staff being left untapped. While it is often helpful and even necessary to bring in outside supports for development, we should consider the value of peer-to-peer learning as part of our staff development plan. If we have hired well, we will be surrounded by smart, capable, and competent individuals.

In our organization, we are constantly looking for creative ways that we can learn from each other. As part of our staff's development each year, we gather off-site for a day of professional development. We have also found it valuable for employees with highly developed skill sets in a particular area to provide internal training to their coworkers. Our staff have provided mini presentations on a variety of topics such as advanced use of Microsoft Excel, project management, and using social media. The idea is to learn from each other and celebrate the diversity of our team.

Many people are happiest when they are learning and growing – this is part of human nature. We all want to feel the satisfaction of getting better and developing our skills, and when we do this together it creates a culture of development. By helping staff recognize that every person on their team has a unique contribution from which they can benefit and learn, we can continue to learn and grow together as an organization.

REFLECTION QUESTIONS

1. In your workplace, which has been more prized: individual performance and accountability or group learning and development? What has been the result of this?
2. What are you doing to promote development in your organization? How well are you utilizing the skills of your current staff? How could you more fully capitalize on their skills?

PRACTICAL APPLICATION

Have a conversation with each of your staff members and ask them what area they would like to develop. Then pair them with someone you know will be able to teach them what they would like to learn and have them schedule a training session together.

ADDITIONAL RESOURCE

The Empowerment Manual: A Guide for Collaborative Groups by Starhawk (New Society Publishers, 2011)

32
WHEN LEADERSHIP TRANSITIONS

BY RANDY GRIESER

"Nothing is permanent except change." Mr. Hawkins, my fourth-grade teacher, is the first person I remember using this phrase – and now I use it too. While this statement may be true, change is still difficult, sometimes confusing, and often frustrating for those experiencing it. For organizations, changes that are not implemented well frequently cause stress and increased conflict for staff, which often results in decreased employee engagement and productivity. Given that change is inevitable in any context, it's important to do it well.

One of our most significant changes at ACHIEVE in the last number of years has been a leadership transition. In the summer of 2020, we announced that I would be stepping into my new role of Chief Vision Officer after nearly 15 years as CEO, and our Managing Director, Eric Stutzman, would take my place. This meant that Eric would start providing regular support to the rest of our leadership team and actively managing our day-to-day operations. I would transition to a less hands-on role where I could dedicate my energies more broadly to projects that support our vision of creating workplaces where people like to work, particularly through keynote speaking and overseeing the book projects of our publishing division.

When we made this announcement public, it didn't come as a surprise to anyone in our organization. This was because the steps leading up to it and the communication around the transition had been thoughtfully planned and well-executed. The public announcement was more of a statement of what had already happened, and less about what was to come.

About three years before this formal transition, I had started to think seriously about these changes and knew that it would be critical to our success to plan with intentionality. So, together with our leadership team, we thoughtfully and deliberately put together a plan. From our experience with other changes, both internal and external to our organization, we knew that there were two critical things we needed to do for this to be a smooth transition: *communicate the plan for change early* and *communicate it often.*

We first introduced this plan to staff two years before the formal announcement. The great benefit of the longer timeframe between the announcement and the actual change was that it gave employees time to settle into the idea and get comfortable with it *before* it happened. Following this internal announcement, we slowly started making the changes to our roles. We took our time and frequently communicated with staff about when and why things were happening as they were.

Despite our best intentions, the transition was not always without challenges or confusion. But when these challenges occurred, we were quick to acknowledge that there would be some bumps along the way and that we were always open to questions from staff. We assured everyone we would do our best to work through and address issues as they arose.

While we had planned the communication part of the transition well, the biggest thing we had failed to consider was that the most important question on people's minds during a change is "What does this change mean for me?" When transitions are announced, people are most nervous about the direct effect on them – how they will be personally impacted by the change. As a leadership team, it became

When transitions are announced, people are most nervous about the direct effect on them – how they will be personally impacted by the change.

___

clear that this was the question we needed to pay closer attention to as our transition continued. Digging deeper into this concern, we learned that the main cause of stress was related to the future change in reporting structures. Many of both mine and Eric's direct reports would now be reporting to other managers.

Once we clued in to this stress, we made sure to provide opportunities for teams and their upcoming new manager to get to know one another. For one team that I had historically led, this included sending them to a two-day conference in order to intentionally get to know each other *without me*. As a result of this type of intentionality, employees and leaders had already begun settling into their new reality over the months leading up to our formalized leadership transition. Thus, the question of "What does this change mean for me?" had, for the most part, been answered *before* the formalization of the transition.

The takeaway from our experience with leadership transitions is equally applicable to most changes. For those of you who are considering a significant transition that will impact a lot of people, I encourage you to consider your approach – don't let it be haphazard. If you are planning for a change, plan early, be methodical, and communicate often. And be mindful of the question on everyone's mind: "What does this change mean for me?"

REFLECTION QUESTIONS

1. Consider a leadership transition you have experienced, either as a staff member or as a leader. How were people impacted? What went well and what didn't with the change?
2. What change are you currently experiencing or planning to implement at your organization? With this change, how are you answering the employee's question of "What does this change mean for me?"

PRACTICAL APPLICATION

The next time your organization is planning a change, schedule a meeting with other leaders to discuss a plan. Talk about how you can communicate this change with employees and be sure to consider how they will be affected. Then get started on discussing the transition with your employees.

ADDITIONAL RESOURCE

Managing Transitions: Making the Most of Change by William Bridges and Susan Bridges (Hachette Books, 2017)

33

TAKE THE LEAD IN
EMOTIONAL AUTHENTICITY

BY ERIC STUTZMAN

Too often I see people at work trying to avoid emotional authenticity, which includes being honest about feelings of discomfort or pain. I believe this is a roadblock to relationship building. Being open about our emotions – *including* pain – allows us to be true to who we are, develop trust, and build healthy relationships with each other. In order for everyone to express their emotions in the workplace, leaders need to create an environment where people feel safe enough to be vulnerable. When we develop safety – when people know they are honored and respected for who they are as whole people – we create the conditions for emotional expression and the development of authentic relationships.

Our staff recently experienced a conversation that required emotional authenticity. For context, Canada, where I live, has a long and painful history of oppressing the Indigenous peoples who live here, and in recent years has engaged in a reconciliation process that has led to the Truth and Reconciliation Commission of Canada's Calls to Action. Our organization has committed to walking the path of reconciliation and responding to the Calls to Action. As part of our response, we brought our staff together for a training session and conversation about reconciliation.

We invited one of our trainers, Noela Crowe-Salazar, to lead the session. As an Indigenous person, she shared her family's story with us and how she was the first child in four generations *not* to be taken away to a residential school before the age of six. I couldn't help but think about my own children – my own six-year-old – and how devastating it would be for her and our family if she were forcibly removed from our home, taken off to boarding school, and forced to assimilate to a new culture. I imagined what it would be like to not see her or even communicate with her for months at a time. I felt that pain, and I was deeply moved. I'm still deeply moved.

Noela also told us stories of strength, healing, resilience, and hope. And then each person who was there had the opportunity to respond to what we heard, to situate our own stories into the greater narrative. We felt safe enough to be authentic and share deeply with each other.

The emotional authenticity we experienced with each other that day had several positive impacts. First, we trust each other more. I also understand my colleagues more fully because I have seen and experienced more of their humanity – their hurt and their hope. Through our listening, we also discovered that we could relate to each other's experiences. This allows us to communicate more openly and directly with one another, which means we can work more effectively as a team.

SURVEY QUOTE
Vulnerability is a necessary quality for effective leadership as it gives the leader a realness and helps develop trust and loyalty.

I have often seen that people avoid discussing and feeling hard emotions at work because leaders have not made it safe enough to do so. People do not want to be vulnerable or share their difficulties when they are worried about their reputation, gossip, or a lack of confidentiality. No one wants to be judged, but guardedness has serious downsides. Among them, it means that we are not able to communicate as effectively with each other.

As leaders, we are tasked with creating environments where people are psychologically safe. Not only is this a legal requirement in many places, but it also makes good sense from an organizational and purely human point of view. When people are safe, they build strong relationships and flourish. All of this contributes to thriving organizations.

Although we can work at building psychological safety through our policies, it can be practically applied every time a team gathers to discuss topics that matter to people. Based on our experiences, I want to offer you four simple ways to create safety for times when your team gathers to discuss or process challenging topics.

Leaders Go First

Although it is not always best for a leader to speak first, when it comes to vulnerability, they should be the first to say something. By demonstrating that they are willing to be humble, honest, and emotionally transparent, they make it safer for everyone else to do the same.

Honor Each Other's Stories

Before having a conversation that brings up emotions or personal sharing, people need to know how their information will be treated. One simple way to establish healthy confidentiality is to propose to the group that any story belongs to the storyteller. Each person in the group who heard the story can share in the lessons of the story, but unless they have permission, they will not discuss the details with others.

Sit With the Pain

In any group, there will be some who want to fix other people's struggles or pain by offering them solutions. Although this may come with good intentions, it is often experienced as unhelpful, minimizing, or patronizing. Leaders should explain that if someone shares something that is hard, it is more helpful to sit with the story and feel it with them than it is to try and fix it – listening and simply being together is enough.

Ask What It Means

We have a deeply held desire to make meaning of pain or suffering. When we experience difficult emotions or experiences, one of the most helpful things we can do is ask what it means for us. Sometimes that meaning making leads us to acceptance, sometimes it prompts us to act. From a workplace perspective, we can ask what the experience we are discussing means to us in terms of our purpose or mission. This helps focus the team on actions that relate to the organization's work.

I do not believe that we should intentionally seek painful or difficult experiences to discuss unless the topic is connected to our work. Instead, we should focus on accepting that they will arise from time to time. When they do, leaders should focus on establishing safety for the conversations so that we can be vulnerable, make meaning, and move to action. In doing so, we create the conditions for strong relationships that will ultimately strengthen our work.

REFLECTION QUESTIONS

1. Think about a time when you have been with a group of people where it felt safe to be emotionally authentic with each other. What was that like for you? What was the result?
2. Consider the culture of your organization when it comes to emotional authenticity. When someone shares something that is difficult or vulnerable, is their story honored? What more could you and other leaders do to be more authentic and to invite the same from staff?

PRACTICAL APPLICATION

Consider the ways in which you can contribute to creating an emotionally open and safe workplace. The next time you have a meeting in which you are talking about something impactful to the team, follow through with one or two strategies that will either model, affirm, or create a safe space for people to be emotionally open.

ADDITIONAL RESOURCE

The Art of Authenticity: Tools to Become an Authentic Leader and Your Best Self by Karissa Thacker (Wiley, 2016)

34

FOCUS ON CULTURE, NOT PERKS

BY RANDY GRIESER

I occasionally read the results of various awards for "The Best Places to Work" or "Top Employers" with cynical interest. These awards are typically given out by various business and national media publications, and while the intent to highlight great workplaces has merit, it is what is measured that I take exception to. Most of these publications highlight statistics and stories about perks like free lunches, pet-friendly offices, free childcare, beer fridges, nap rooms, and unlimited time off. When reading about the winners, it seems that awards are essentially given out to the organizations that have the best or most perks.

Although perks may sound great and can help employees feel good about their workplace some of the time, the truth is that they only get at a small part of what makes a workplace great. While they are enjoyable to have, and perhaps even helpful, they are almost meaningless in the absence of a healthy workplace culture. For example, all the perks in the world won't make up for having a manager who treats staff poorly or help an employee feel good about work when they have to regularly deal with toxic conflict. Perks may keep an employee who finds their tasks meaningless and unfulfilling engaged for a while, but their motivation and interest in the workplace will eventually decrease.

A healthy workplace culture will cultivate more employee engagement, better performance, and higher productivity than perks.

Through my own experiences, research, and interviews with others, I've found that a far better measuring stick for determining what makes a workplace great is culture, not perks. A healthy workplace culture will cultivate more employee engagement, better performance, and higher productivity than perks. In our book, *The Culture Question*, my co-authors and I outline six key pillars of a healthy workplace culture. These are the areas that leaders have the power and responsibility to prioritize over perks.

Communicate Your Purpose and Values

Employees are inspired when they work in organizations where the purpose and values resonate with them. Does everyone in your workplace know and understand its purpose and values? Once the values are identified, focus on helping employees connect the way they work to the values of the organization and the contribution of their work to the organization's greater purpose.

Provide Meaningful Work

Most employees want to work on projects that inspire them, align with what they are good at, and allow them to grow. How much attention has your workplace given to making sure that everyone has meaningful work? Organizations should be intentional about finding each person's true talents and giving them work that builds on those talents and provides them with a sense of satisfaction.

Focus Your Leadership Team on People

How leaders relate to employees plays a major role in how each person feels about their workplace. Are your organization's leaders sufficiently aware of how they impact others in the workplace? Focus on teaching leaders to care about staff as people and support them in their work while providing healthy levels of accountability.

Build Meaningful Relationships

When employees like the people they work with and for, they are more satisfied and engaged in their work. How strong are the relationships within your workplace? Organizations should focus on building an environment in which relationships can grow and people can connect with each other across teams.

Create Peak Performing Teams

People are energized when they work together effectively because teams achieve things that no one person could do on their own. How well do people at your organization work together in team environments? Workplaces should focus on helping staff collaborate with each other, building diversity into teams, and capitalizing on collective intelligence.

Practice Constructive Conflict Management

When leaders don't handle conflict quickly and effectively, it promptly sours the workplace. How skilled are employees and managers when it comes to working through conflict? Organizations should focus on training people to resolve differences quickly and directly.

SURVEY STATISTICS

There were significant differences between those who reported having a healthy workplace culture and those who said theirs is unhealthy:

SURVEY STATEMENT	Percentage of those who agreed with the survey statement *and* said their workplace has a *healthy* culture.	Percentage of those who agreed with the survey statement *and* said their workplace has an *unhealthy* culture.
Leaders in my organization demonstrate care for their staff.	87%	24%
My organization values leadership development.	86%	38%
When the world outside of my organization changes, our leaders are quick to adapt.	79%	28%
There is a high level of trust between staff and leaders in my organization.	68%	4%

As leaders, we play a critical role in shaping our organization's culture – and 96 percent of our survey respondents agree with this. The many benefits of a healthy workplace culture mean we should give it the attention it needs to flourish. If our culture is healthy, engagement, performance, and productivity will be high (see Survey Statistics above). If it's weak, no number of free lunches or beer fridges will make up for it. Organizations that live out these six pillars of a healthy workplace culture are far more worthy of winning awards than those who offer perks. The good news is that while culture requires attention and intentionality, you don't need a budget for perks to improve it.

REFLECTION QUESTIONS

1. How has your organization viewed the relationship between perks and being a great place to work? Where has it put its attention?
2. Which of the six pillars of healthy workplace culture does your organization already do well? Which pillars require your attention moving forward?

PRACTICAL APPLICATION

Complete ACHIEVE's free Workplace Cultural Health Assessment found in the Free Resources section of our website (www.achievecentre.com) and discuss the findings with others in your organization. This assessment normally takes between two and five minutes to complete. You will be provided with an eight-page report that will help you evaluate, understand, and discuss your organization's culture.

ADDITIONAL RESOURCE

The Culture Question: How to Create a Workplace Where People Like to Work by Randy Grieser, Eric Stutzman, Wendy Loewen, and Michael Labun (ACHIEVE Publishing, 2019)

35

LET'S TALK ABOUT THE ELEPHANT IN THE ROOM

BY ERIC STUTZMAN

I've facilitated a number of high-stakes conversations over the years and am always struck when organizations ask me to lead a discussion about the elephant in the room. Rather than needing help with a conflict or to identify specific problems, they are simply asking me to start a conversation about a problem they are all aware of but can't seem to talk about.

In one case, the shareholders of a private company had avoided talking about a major ownership issue for several years that was likely causing them to lose ground in the market. The "elephant" that they were avoiding could have lost them tens of millions of dollars per year and would have affected the livelihood of many employees. The shareholders, who all owned different percentages of the company, were telling me privately that they wanted to know what others were thinking. As the facilitator, I knew that those with fewer shares were afraid of what the bigger shareholders might want, and that the bigger shareholders also wanted to know what the smaller ones were thinking. Each group had fears about bringing up the issue.

So why do we sometimes avoid talking about the big issues, whether in our personal lives or at work? Why do we avoid telling an employee about a performance issue, talking about an office romance that is creating a disturbance, or discussing something important at our leadership meetings? Think back to a time when you did not talk about a big issue and see if these common concerns were true for you:

- I did not want to offend anyone or have anyone be upset with me.
- I was afraid of starting a conflict.
- I did not know how to talk about the elephant in the room.
- I was worried it would affect my career.
- I was not sure I or the other person could handle the outcome.

The first two reasons are often connected – when we have serious concerns about an issue, we fear the risk associated with talking about it. We do not want to escalate conflict or break the fragile balance that may exist in the way our relationship is currently functioning. In the instance with the shareholders, the status quo was working *okay*, and people feared upsetting the current balance that brought in a reasonable amount of profit.

SURVEY QUOTE
A good leader is someone who has the courage to openly discuss awkward or difficult issues with all staff.

The problem is that when we fear talking about something and choose to stay silent, one of two things will happen: we will eventually talk about our fears (often in less-than-ideal ways); or we act on them in ways that may have unintentional consequences. The fear of talking about something directly often leads to whispered side conversations, passive-aggressive behavior, and avoidance – all of which get in the way of growth. We often know there is an elephant in the room because of these behaviors.

Although thinking through the potential costs of speaking about the elephant in the room is important, we should all consider the costs of *not* discussing it. This often provides the motivation we need to voice our opinions. For example, if you avoid talking to an employee about a performance issue, it may affect the quality of services you offer and be a detriment to the organization. Additionally, this is unfair to the employee if they are unaware of the issue. In the case of the shareholders, not talking meant lost opportunity – potentially millions of dollars of lost income.

When you compare the cost of bringing up an issue to that of remaining silent, you will often find that the risk of not talking about it is greater. When you realize this, it is time to act. There are four things to remember as you prepare to talk about the elephant in the room.

1. State Your Positive Intentions

When you begin the conversation, it is important to explain your positive intentions for bringing up the issue. This is because others will likely be fearful about discussing it. They may worry that talking about what has never been discussed will create problems. Before you start, ask yourself what positive things you hope to achieve by discussing the elephant in the room. Do you want to solve a longstanding issue? Do you want to create understanding? Name your intention as you start the conversation.

2. Get Ready to Listen

We are used to preparing ourselves to talk or even argue about big issues. But what really needs to happen when there is an elephant in the room is for everyone to understand each other before making decisions. The only way to reach understanding effectively is to actively listen. This means beginning the conversation by asking people open-ended questions about what they see or experience. Preparing yourself to listen also means being ready to verbally summarize what you have heard others say so that they know they have been heard and understood. When you do this, you create the conditions for them to listen to you at the same time.

3. Discuss the Facts
Remember that it is much easier to discuss a shared problem when we focus on starting with the facts or what people have observed. Instead of focusing on the reasons why people may or may not have done things, focus on what has actually happened or is currently happening. Then discuss the impact of what is happening and your worries and hopes for the future. If you focus on facts and on impact, you will create understanding and thus reduce the defensiveness of everyone involved in the conversation.

4. Ask For Help If Needed
Big issues often go unaddressed for a long time. Perhaps you already tried to talk about an issue, but it did not go well and added to the fear of bringing it up again. Or maybe those within your organization are finding it difficult to get enough distance from the issue to start the conversation. When an elephant seems too big to tackle on your own, it can be helpful to hire a trained coach, facilitator, or mediator. Outside help will bring good questions to the conversation, keep track of important information, and help everyone listen to each other by creating a safe process for discussion.

I have come to know that our fear of what people might say about the elephant in the room is largely misplaced. What we *should* fear is the lack of information caused by not talking. A lack of communication is what leads us to make bad decisions or inhibits our growth. So, go ahead and talk about the elephant in the room – doing so will enable you to develop deeper insights into your situation, make better decisions, and grow.

REFLECTION QUESTIONS

1. Consider a time when an important issue wasn't discussed at your organization. What were the consequences of not talking about it?

2. Are there any current issues that aren't being talked about in your organization? What would happen if you and others focused on the cost of not talking about the issue(s)? What are your options for starting a discussion about the elephant in the room that would make people more receptive to the conversation?

PRACTICAL APPLICATION

The next time you notice people are not talking about something important, pause to consider the costs of not bringing it up. Ask those who should be involved in the conversation if it might be useful to talk about the issue or note that there may be a cost to not talking about it. Then ask a question and be prepared to listen.

ADDITIONAL RESOURCE

Difficult Conversations: How to Discuss What Matters Most by Douglas Stone, Bruce Patton, and Sheila Heen (Penguin Books, 2010)

36
HARNESSING THE POWER
OF AFFIRMATION

BY WENDY LOEWEN

As a teenager I spent the summer months at country fairs competing in horse shows. In preparation for the upcoming show season each spring, a small group of us young horse enthusiasts would have a week of intense training. One coach in particular stands out as exceptional. Under his guidance I was inspired to work hard and improve my skills. One of the most powerful things he did was provide detailed affirmation when he saw us doing something that worked.

In one particular lesson we were working on sliding stops – this is when a horse is in a full gallop and comes to a sudden stop. The horse plants their hind feet on the ground and then allows them to slide for several feet as they continue to "walk" their front legs forward. Our coach gave us instruction and then left us to practice on our own. When we regrouped, he asked each one of us to demonstrate. When it was my turn, I was nervous to be put on the spot. But to my surprise, my horse and I did an amazing job! I don't remember exactly what he said, but it went something like this: "Great job, Wendy. You got up to a good speed, pushed down with your seat, leaned back, gently dropped your heels down, and moved your legs away from the horse's side. That is how we get the results we will need in the show ring."

Part of the reason his affirmation was so powerful was its specificity.

It wasn't simply, "Good job!" He clearly outlined what I had done well and what I needed to continue doing to get the outcome that I wanted. This learning can be applied to our role as leaders as well. By providing our staff with specific affirmations when we recognize noteworthy contributions, we help people identify what they are doing to produce quality work and outline what we want them to continue doing.

Positive feedback is a powerful way to enhance learning and performance, and specific affirmations capitalize on this. People like to hear when they are doing a good job and to know that their work is of value. It makes them feel good, increases their satisfaction, and energizes them to continue their efforts. It also communicates that we are paying attention as we speak to the desired actions needed for organizational success.

I have come to believe that the behaviors we affirm should be where excellent work or effort are demonstrated. We certainly do not want to affirm mediocre efforts or contributions. If we do, we are sure to continue to get mediocrity in return. When looking for specific behaviors to affirm, I have found that there are five key ways to contribute to organizational success that should be validated.

Acting on Organizational Values

When staff act on an organizational value, it provides a key opportunity to offer affirmation because it reinforces the continual embrace of these values. For example, one of our organization's values is "flexibility." Recently I noticed that one of our staff had a stack of filing on her desk that she wasn't able to tackle as she was dealing with another pressing work-related issue. I asked another employee if they would be willing to pitch in. She happily complied and jumped in to lend a hand. By being flexible and completing a task that wasn't her direct responsibility, she gave her coworker some much-needed support. This was the perfect opportunity for me to offer a specific validation as she clearly demonstrated her willingness to be flexible.

Positive feedback is a powerful way to enhance learning and performance, and specific affirmations capitalize on this.

Following Processes and Procedures Carefully

Take note when people complete tasks exactly as expected and outlined in their job description or procedural requirements. Recently I overheard someone on our leadership team verbally affirm the attention to detail that a staff member had taken in creating a spreadsheet. The data was well researched, accurate, and delivered on time, and the supervisor took the time to acknowledge the staff member's meticulous work. Her careful attention to detail ensured we were able to make a decision based on an accurate assessment of the situation. When we affirm and acknowledge an employee's good work, it makes them feel valued and that their extra efforts are worth it. It also encourages them to deliver high-quality work in the future. And, in this case, the specific affirmation encouraged the staff member to continue giving the focus needed to complete her tasks well.

Creatively Completing Tasks

Be on the lookout for those who produce high-quality work with the use of creativity, ingenuity, or out-of-the-box thinking. Several months ago, one of our staff added color and created a visually striking document with graphs and charts when I had asked for a simple black and white document with the data in bullet points. Her work went above and beyond my expectations. When the client commented on how well the document was put together, it reminded me that this was an opportunity to validate the innovative work that led to a high-quality finished product. This affirmation spurred her on to continue her creative work, and since then she has created several new templates that were spin-offs from her original work.

Persisting in the Face of Barriers

When we see that an employee's work is on track despite facing obstacles, we have an opportunity to provide affirmation. This kind of affirmation helps staff see that their persistence has value and motivates them to keep working, even when there are challenges. Barriers may be a shortage of time, a demanding client, or lack of resources where we simply cannot provide more. When we see that our staff are working hard to keep up, learn a new task, or deal with unplanned interruptions, we should see this as a chance to affirm their determination and persistence. Recently a new hire expressed that they were struggling to learn one of our systems. I asked them to share what they were doing to learn the complicated system, and their response made it clear that they had spent hours researching and exploring the system and had already made significant inroads in their understanding. With a bit of specific affirmation, they realized that their effort was appreciated, they could take pride in how far they had come, and they were motivated to dive back in with renewed energy.

Demonstrating Reliability

Take time to offer a specific affirmation when you see that an employee has demonstrated loyalty, reliability, or consistency. In our workplaces we need to rely on staff to consistently show up and to do their best work in order to deliver quality services and products – even on tasks that are not exciting. It is important for leaders to remember that even employees whose tasks require them to do repetitive work deserve to be praised. In our organization we typically have several data collection projects on the go. Although the work is not exciting, it contributes greatly to our success. Our leadership team intentionally affirms those staff who spend time on these projects. They note specifically how the project contributes to our organizational success. This kind of affirmation can go a long way toward motivating staff as they complete tasks, even when they are mundane.

We all want to know that our contributions matter and that we are appreciated. Specific verbal affirmation is a simple way to acknowledge and express appreciation for our staff and their work. This type of recognition builds a drive to excel, motivates performance, and improves confidence, which ultimately enhances overall organizational success. Specific affirmation is simple to implement and doesn't cost anything other than our attention, and the returns remind us that it is a powerful leadership tool.

REFLECTION QUESTIONS

1. In what ways have you been supporting the efforts of your staff or team members with specific affirmations? What is the last affirmation you have given and how was it received?
2. As you consider the culture of your organization, where does affirmation fit? What opportunities do you see for building more affirmation into your work as a leader?

PRACTICAL APPLICATION

Write down the names of staff who look to you for direction, as well as other colleagues who may benefit from receiving positive feedback from you. As you go through your week, observe their efforts and contributions, and commit to offering each person at least one specific affirmation. This can be done in the moment, or you can plan where and when you will give the affirmation.

ADDITIONAL RESOURCE

Leading with Gratitude: Eight Leadership Practices for Extraordinary Business Results by Adrian Gostick and Chester Elton (Harper Business, 2020)

37

MOVING PROJECTS FORWARD

BY RANDY GRIESER

I've always lived by the principle that *if you aren't five minutes early, you're already late.* When my wife and I are meeting friends for supper, I'm always pushing her to leave a little early, just to make sure we're on time. While attending university, I never pulled an all-nighter writing a paper. My desire to finish my papers by the deadline meant organizing my schedule so I would finish the paper well before the due date. And in my current work, if a project or task has been highlighted as valuable to us – even in a small way – the task is almost always finished early.

This way of thinking and planning is even more critical for larger scale projects that take a long time to complete. I've learned that, as an organization, most of the important things we do are not accomplished in a day or two, but rather require committed energy and focus over very long periods of time – months and even years of work. And to do these projects well – to start them, work through challenges and difficulties, and then finally finish them – requires methodical planning and focus. This requires simultaneously working on parts of the project today, while also keeping the long-term goal in mind.

Writing a book is a good example of this type of project. One of my primary tasks outside of writing and speaking is to oversee all our book projects through our publishing division, ACHIEVE Publishing. Most book projects I've been a part of have taken about two years to plan, write, edit, design, and print. Finishing a book (let alone finishing it on time) doesn't happen without careful and methodical planning. Key to meeting our end goal has been our ability to meet deadlines that have been established for multiple checkpoints along the way. I know very well that if part of the large-scale project gets delayed, it will have a ripple effect on the other checkpoints, and the final deadline will be in danger of being missed. In short, what we do or *don't do* today has an impact on our ability to finish a project on time.

Recently I had some pushback from a member of our team related to a new book project that is in the early stages of the process. We are far enough along that various checkpoints have been established, and we know when we want the book finished. We were having difficulty finding a time when all members of the project could meet to discuss an issue that needed to be resolved before moving the book forward. This particular member didn't feel the same sense of urgency I and others had and asked, "What's the rush on needing to meet right away? Why can't we just talk in a few weeks when everyone has more time?" In short, she was saying that we had a lot of time to write the book, so we didn't need to be so worried about meeting right away. I quickly put on my strategic planning hat and gently reminded her that what we do or don't do today will impact our ability to actually finish this project on time. I briefly outlined the ripple effect of not meeting. Through this discussion she quickly realized the long-term impact of not meeting. After a bit more effort we were able to find a time to meet that worked for all of us.

What we do or don't do *today has an impact on our ability to finish a project on time.*

As leaders we play an important role in ensuring a large project happens on time and as planned. After being a part of many larger projects that require years to accomplish, I've come to see that a leader has three key tasks when it comes to managing projects: set expectations, give inspiration, and provide accountability.

Set Expectations and Timelines

Starting with a detailed plan that includes project leaders, action items, and timelines is crucial for the success of most projects, big or small. And equally as important is to *write the plan down*. Saving the plan on a computer is fine, but in any big project I'm involved with, I have the plan printed off and taped on my office wall where I can look at it regularly. Keeping the plan front and center better allows you to refer to it often, which will help you stay on track and meet your deadlines. If a bigger project isn't planned well from the start, rest assured that issues that would have been navigable with a plan can potentially derail the project and prevent it from being completed.

Give Inspiration

At the start of a project, there is often positive energy that will naturally push it forward for a few months. However, there will inevitably come a time when people lose ambition, become frustrated, or lose focus, and the project momentum slows down or, at worst, stalls. This is when the team members need to hear from you, their leader, so you can remind them of the project's importance. Remind people of the final vision of the project and be sure to explain how it connects with the purpose, vision, and values of your organization. One practical way I've found helpful for giving inspiration is to pause and celebrate project milestones. This helps to acknowledge what's been done so far, but also serves to inspire staff to move on to the next phase.

Provide Accountability

At the start of the project, be sure to communicate that any delay to the plan will have major ripple effects. I have found it helpful to intentionally connect with people a few weeks before a checkpoint to remind them I will be doing a formal check-in soon. For anyone who has fallen behind, this is a good reminder to get moving and finish their part of the project before the next deadline. If a person or team is struggling to meet deadlines, determine what the issue is and fix it. It may be a skill set is missing and a new team member is needed, workloads are too heavy, or they don't have the right tools. Another way that is helpful to provide accountability is to have check-ins as a whole group. The timing of this will be different for each team and project – it may be weekly, monthly, or quarterly. Having conversations collectively also helps to foster peer accountability.

Most of the meaningful or important things we accomplish are only achieved through continuous and focused effort. When leaders ensure projects start with a clear plan, give inspiration throughout the process, and provide accountability to team members, they are much more likely to be done well and on time.

REFLECTION QUESTIONS

1. What has been your experience when leading large projects? What has worked well and what hasn't?
2. In what ways are you effective at setting expectations, giving inspiration, and providing accountability on the projects you lead? How could you do better in these areas?

PRACTICAL APPLICATION

Consider a project you are just starting or are in the midst of. How have you or how do you plan to set expectations, give inspiration, and provide accountability? Make sure the plan is written down, and if it's not your practice already, try printing the plan off and putting it on your wall.

ADDITIONAL RESOURCE

Harvard Business Review Project Management Handbook: How to Launch, Lead, and Sponsor Successful Projects by Antonio Nieto-Rodriguez (Harvard Business Review Press, 2021)

38

WHAT ARE YOUR WORKPLACE RITUALS?

BY ERIC STUTZMAN

When a new employee starts in our organization, we have a welcoming ritual. Everyone gathers for coffee and snacks at some point during the employee's first week. We gather in a circle and each person introduces the person next to them by identifying some of their strengths and something fun about them that isn't related to work. Although the mechanics of this have changed a little as we have grown, the essentials have not. We enjoy food together, and we celebrate each other's strengths and quirks.

Rituals are defining events that repeat themselves in the life cycle of an organization, and they reflect and communicate its values and priorities in powerful ways. For example, if an organization values responding positively to feedback, sharing a story about learning from criticism at each staff meeting shows people just how closely this value is held. If an organization values strong interpersonal relationships, a ritual of getting together for food and connection communicates this more strongly than words on a page ever could.

In their article, "Want to Strengthen Workplace Culture? Design a Ritual," Mollie West and Kate McCoubrey Judson explain that "Rituals engage people around the things that matter most to an organization, instilling a sense of shared purpose and experience. They spark behaviors that make the work and the company more successful."[1] In addition to showing what kind of behavior is valued, rituals help build camaraderie and they give us a sense that we belong to a unique and special group. After our own welcoming ritual, new employees feel like they are becoming part of a team that enjoys and values one another.

Rituals vary in scope and complexity. They may be simple like always starting your staff meetings with a joke, or everyone crafting their email signature in a unique way. Or they may be complex, built around how you celebrate personal or organizational milestones – things like attending the same charity fundraisers every year, storytelling rituals at holiday parties, or even organized potlucks.

Often rituals begin without a lot of forethought. We try something, people like it, and then we repeat it. But I believe that creating rituals with intention can add a lot of value to them. Given the way rituals reinforce values and beliefs, we should pay attention to creating rituals that emphasize the values that are important to our organizations. For instance, one of our values is being *engaged* – we care about our mission and each other. This value is reinforced by rituals like our welcoming circle.

We must also remember that our rituals should serve a positive purpose for our organizations. It's easy to continue rituals without changing them, even when they are no longer fun or serving their original purpose. Our own welcoming circle ritual began when we had about eight staff members. It created a sense of inclusion, camaraderie, and humor. At that time, our tradition was to ask the second most recent hire to introduce everyone in the circle to the newest staff member. But once we hit 15+ employees, I started hearing that it was becoming more intimidating and less enjoyable (for some), and I certainly noticed that it was more time consuming. Since our intention was to be welcoming and put people at ease, we adapted our ritual to have each employee introduce the person beside them.

Rituals sometimes seem untouchable, as though we can't alter them because that would ruin their importance. However, like all aspects

In addition to showing what kind of behavior is valued, rituals help build camaraderie and they give us a sense that we belong to a unique and special group.

of organizational culture, we should expect our rituals to evolve over time. As our organizations change, and as our people change, so should our rituals. Here are some ideas to help you determine how well your rituals fit with your organization's culture:

List Your Rituals

If you have a hard time identifying your organization's rituals, it might be time to start some. Remember, rituals include things like how you celebrate personal or organizational milestones, annual events like charity fundraisers, and eating together. Rituals are built by repetition, so if you try something and it works, repeat it.

Ensure Your Intentions Match Their Impact

Make sure you consider the newest and least powerful people as you think about the impact of your rituals, as it is usually people in these roles that are first to feel the negative impact of poorly conceived rituals. In our case, our welcoming ritual became more uncomfortable for our newest staff as we got larger, especially for those who were less inclined to speak in front of a group. If the effect is different than your intention, consider adjusting the ritual.

Ensure Your Rituals Communicate Your Values

Rituals tell staff what is important, what you laugh about, or where you spend your energy in your organization, much like our welcoming ritual. Consider your organization's stated values. If your rituals don't match your values, look for ways to bring them into alignment. If your organization does not have stated values, then consider what values your rituals communicate and ask yourself if you and the other leaders are comfortable with that.

Our rituals bring a sense of definition and rhythm to our work lives, showing us what the organization and the people around us value. As leaders, we have two options when it comes to rituals: we can let them form on their own, or we can be intentional about starting and shaping them. I believe we should choose the latter option as much as possible because of the way rituals shape and communicate our workplace culture.

REFLECTION QUESTIONS

1. Consider rituals that you have enjoyed either in your current workplace or elsewhere. What did you like about them, and what values did they communicate?
2. Which of your workplace values are currently being reinforced through rituals? What could you and your team do to be more intentional about your rituals?

PRACTICAL APPLICATION

As you move through your week, make a list of the rituals that occur in your workplace. Consider both the simple and more complex rituals. Then identify one that you would like to shift or improve and develop a specific plan to do so over the coming months or year. If you are struggling to identify existing positive rituals, make a plan to establish a ritual for your team that is meaningful, connected to your values, and builds a positive workplace culture.

ADDITIONAL RESOURCE

Rituals Roadmap: The Human Way to Transform Everyday Routines into Workplace Magic by Erica Keswin (McGraw-Hill Education, 2021)

39

CREATING A PSYCHOLOGICALLY SAFE WORKPLACE

BY WENDY LOEWEN

I grew up in the country, which meant that by the time I was 16, I had already logged many hours driving on dirt roads. I was a confident driver but was also a little apprehensive the first time I drove to the city with a friend. Luckily, it was an hour-and-a-half drive, and by the time we rolled into the city limits I was more relaxed. That changed when we started the journey home and a car veered in front of us – I was able to avert a collision but was left terrified and shaking. I pulled onto a side street, parked the car, took a deep breath, and waited for my heart to stop racing.

After a few minutes, I started the car and we headed back home. However, in my anxious state I proceeded the wrong way down a one-way street! It was terrifying to see cars coming toward me, but I quickly realized my mistake and again pulled over to the side of the road. Normally I was a good driver but being cut off had put me in a state of stress and caused my brain to check out. There was a clearly posted sign stating it was a one-way street, but that didn't register for me – all I could think about was getting out of the city and back to safety.

A state of stress causing poor performance isn't unique to driving. When we are fearful, we cannot operate at our full capacity, and we end up functioning with limited brain power. Fear is not just an emotion, but it is also a physical experience. Fear floods our bodies with hormones that prepare us to fight, flight, or freeze, and it deprives our brain of the ability to think clearly. This is true for people in our organization as well – when they are fearful, they cannot function at their best.

Much of the important work in our organizations happens collaboratively. For groups of people working together to be successful, each person needs to access their unique creativity, ingenuity, and problem-solving capacity. And to do so, they must feel safe. This realization should be taken seriously by leaders as we seek to support productivity, innovation, and collaboration; it should propel us to be intentional about creating workplaces that are free of fear.

Many organizations and leaders have begun to recognize the negative effect of fear on their staff's productivity. For example, Google conducted a two-year study on team performance called Project Aristotle. The name of the study is a nod to Aristotle's quote, "The whole is greater than the sum of its parts." The study found that *who* is on a team mattered far less than *how they interact* with each other. They found that one of the most impactful contributors to successful teamwork is the level of psychological safety.[1]

And Google isn't the only one who has found this to be true – the power of psychological safety has been researched and validated by many others, like Amy Edmondson, whose excellent TED Talk, "Building a Psychologically Safe Workplace," was my introduction to the concept. Edmondson defines psychological safety as a team's shared belief that it is safe to take risks with each other. She stresses that it is the leader's role to set the stage for psychological safety to occur on teams and to create a culture of safety. The leader also sets the expectations for how staff will interact and establishes what is safe to reveal, what is safe to discuss, *and* what isn't.[2]

One sign of a psychologically safe workplace is when staff trust that they can approach leaders with any issue that is affecting their ability to perform at work. For example, one of the most difficult topics for staff to talk about is when they are struggling with their mental health. In organizations that are psychologically safe, leaders respond to these and other personal issues with empathy, care, and the appropriate support. Staff know that there will be no negative repercussions or judgment from leaders or others when they bring forward personal issues that are impacting their ability to do their best work.

SURVEY QUOTE

A good leader does not condone or cultivate an atmosphere of fear and intimidation.

One way to assess for psychological safety is to pay attention to how team members interact with each other and leaders. Do they share their opinions freely? Do they raise ideas with each other? Do they quickly admit mistakes? Do they challenge each other's ideas respectfully? Do they affirm each other's diverse experiences and perspectives? When we see these kinds of interactions, we are seeing psychological safety at work. When we don't, we need to consider how we can use our influence as leaders to create greater safety.

Given that we spend approximately 60 percent of our time at work, the psychological safety of our staff and colleagues should be a top priority. In fact, for leaders, it is our responsibility. We know construction sites require hard hats and steel-toed boots and offices have fire extinguishers and first-aid kits because these things prevent or treat physical injuries. So why would we not provide the same "protective gear" for people's psychological well-being? An organization seeking to become more psychologically safe must be proactive in minimizing the risk of psychological injury. This means we should monitor and regularly assess our working conditions, workplace practices, and policies because all of these contribute to our sense of well-being.

Furthermore, a commitment to a psychologically safe workplace needs to be endorsed by all leadership levels, reflected in the organization's values, and illustrated in organizational practices. Leadership teams, starting from the top, need to articulate their commitment to having a psychologically safe workplace and tell staff what steps they are taking to make it so. Then they must follow through on their plans.

Fear debilitates people – on the road and in the workplace. For our organizations to be successful, we need our staff to feel safe so they can do their best work. We want them to fully exercise their creativity, offer distinct perspectives, voice concerns, share ideas even when they are not fully formed, openly speak their mind, and ask for help when they need support.

Although there is no straight path to cultivating psychological safety, it starts with us as leaders. We can begin the journey by providing the safe example that we value when our staff bring issues, questions, and concerns to us. In addition, we should pay attention to the ways in which our teams take risks with each other and then affirm these behaviors. When we do this, we can be confident that we are heading in the right direction as we minimize fear and create a psychologically safe workplace.

REFLECTION QUESTIONS

1. In what ways have you experienced fear as a result of not feeling psychologically safe at work? How did that impact your ability to do your best work?
2. What behaviors do you see that demonstrate psychological safety in your workplace? What behaviors might indicate that people do not feel psychologically safe?

PRACTICAL APPLICATION

Watch Amy Edmondson's TED Talk, "Building a Psychologically Safe Workplace," with your staff. Also consider taking an assessment to evaluate your workplace's level of psychological safety. Discuss your understanding of mental health and well-being with your leadership team and whether you and your staff need training. Then, gather all staff and leaders and share your commitment to creating an organization where people are free to contribute their best work and ask for psychological support when they need it.

ADDITIONAL RESOURCES

The Fearless Organization: Creating Psychological Safety in the Workplace for Learning, Innovation, and Growth by Amy Edmondson (Wiley, 2018)

TED Talk: "Building a Psychologically Safe Workplace" by Amy Edmondson

40

WHAT I LEARNED ABOUT PURPOSE FROM PATAGONIA

BY RANDY GRIESER

I love outdoor activities. Throughout the year I regularly canoe, camp, and hike. In fact, I'm writing this a day after hiking up to a mountain peak. Connected to these activities is my appreciation for quality outdoor clothing purchased from companies who are conscious of the environment.

Over the last few years, I have narrowed my focus to one company from which most of my outdoor clothing purchases are made: Patagonia. My fondness for Patagonia became cemented a few years ago after a visit to one of their outlets. On a busy retail street where rent is extremely high, I walked into the store and wasn't met with clothing or gear, but a *story*. Front and center was a literal storyboard of who Patagonia is and what they believe. Before shopping, I read through their story, which included their purpose: "We're in business to save our home planet."

As I shopped and moved on to the day's other activities, I couldn't shake the impact of this experience. I was struck by how rare it is for me to engage with a brand or organization and really understand why they do what they do – let alone be inspired by it.

This is a great lesson about the importance of having an inspirational purpose and sharing it. This is not news, though. For over a decade now, Simon Sinek's TED Talk, "How Great Leaders Inspire Action," and his book, *Start with Why: How Great Leaders Inspire Everyone to Take Action*, have been key resources for leaders who want to talk about their organization's central purpose. Here's a summary of his thinking on purpose:

> Very few people or companies can clearly articulate WHY they do WHAT they do ... By WHY I mean what is your purpose, cause or belief? WHY does your company exist? ... And WHY should anyone care?[1]

Many readers will be familiar with Sinek's call to "start with why," but how well are you doing at actually turning it into action? Is your organization's purpose inspirational and are you truly communicating it effectively?

In my view, Patagonia is a great example of an organization that has done this effectively. And one of the results is that they have a loyal customer – me – who raves about them (and I'm not the only one). They have a purpose I'm inspired by, believe in, and actually know about! It's not hidden on some back page of their website or stuck behind a clothing rack on an engraved brass plate in their stores. It's front and center, not just words on an internal document. When you read Patagonia founder Yvon Chouinard's book, *Let My People Go Surfing: The Education of a Reluctant Businessman*, dig deeper into the company's history and values, or listen to stories of others inspired by Patagonia, you can sense that their purpose rings true – it's not just marketing.

In our own organization, we have worked hard to emulate what Patagonia has done. In the introduction and throughout this book, you will often see us reference our purpose and belief that everyone should be able to like where they work. Said a different way, *we're in business to create workplaces where people like to work*. Everything we do – our resources, books, and training materials – is aimed at fulfilling this purpose. We also work hard to regularly communicate our purpose, intentionally and authentically. We share videos focused on our purpose, offer free resources related to it, and you will see it listed prominently on our website.

It's important to note that purpose doesn't just matter to clients – it also matters to staff. One reason for this is because a common purpose gives employees a reason to engage with their work, no matter what they are doing. Several years ago, I asked one of our very involved employees why she was so engaged. One of the things she said was, "Whether I'm entering data, packing a box, or creating an ad, I understand how my work fits into the purpose of our organization." Her response has always served as a vivid reminder of how critical it is that I continue to connect the daily, sometimes mundane work that people do to the purpose of our organization.

SURVEY QUOTE

A leader who is able to create a collective sense of purpose will always succeed.

I have become more mindful of opportunities to bridge connections between what we do day-to-day and how that impacts and fits with our purpose. We often begin meetings by asking questions like, "How does this project impact our purpose?" In performance review meetings, we ask questions like, "How are you contributing to our organization's purpose?" Purpose is not something that we only talk about once a year. Rather, it is a beacon of inspiration and a pillar that provides focus in our daily work and decision-making.

As leaders, we should be passionate about our purpose and sharing our excitement everywhere we can – particularly when we have opportunities to do so in person. Very few people have ever been inspired by an organization's purpose without a leader who is also passionate about it. If we want employees to be excited about our purpose and in turn their contribution to it, it must begin with us. And when we do this well, people will feel valued and as though they belong, and inspired to work alongside us toward that shared purpose.

REFLECTION QUESTIONS

1. What organization's purpose inspires you and why? How does your organization's purpose compare to theirs? Does your purpose inspire people in the same way?
2. How are you communicating your organization's or team's purpose to staff, clients, customers, or those you serve? What more could you do to communicate your purpose?

PRACTICAL APPLICATION

The next time you check in with an employee, either show them how what they do is connected to your organization's purpose, or ask: "How are you contributing to our organization's purpose?" If you work in a large organization, start with how they contribute to their team's purpose, and then move to how they can connect with the larger purpose.

ADDITIONAL RESOURCES

Let My People Go Surfing: The Education of a Reluctant Businessman by Yvon Chouinard (Penguin Books, 2006)

TED Talk: "How Great Leaders Inspire Action" by Simon Sinek

41
GET SERIOUS ABOUT HAVING FUN AT WORK

BY ERIC STUTZMAN

I knew I was going to like my new workplace when, during my job interview, I was asked if I could sing. I answered yes, to which the interviewers exclaimed, "Good, because it's the boss's birthday and we're going to sing Happy Birthday!" And that's exactly what happened. In came the cake, and I sang along with my soon-to-be colleagues. What that moment signaled to me was that this workplace was going to be fun and that the people liked each other – it was something I wanted to be a part of.

When we have fun at work, when we play or do our work in ways that bring us joy, we experience many benefits both personally and professionally. To begin with, having fun reduces our stress. When we are less stressed, we feel better and can focus more effectively as a result. Playfulness involves using creative parts of our brain and improves our learning environment, which can enhance our ability to be creative with our work tasks. Having fun together builds our ability to trust each other and strengthens friendships. All these things – lowered stress, enhanced creativity, increased trust, and stronger friendships – are directly connected to doing better work.

While many people can appreciate the concept of having fun at work, play is not something we normally associate with work. In fact, we usually think of play as the opposite. I know some leaders who react negatively to the term as it relates to work because it reminds them of childishness. However, I think it's worth thinking about play in the context of work because of the benefits it brings to our organizations. Think about play as something we do for enjoyment. It can be anything from thinking in creative ways, doing tasks that we like, communicating with humor, or tossing a ball while discussing a problem. Many of the things we do at work can be enjoyable or done in fun ways, especially when they connect with our strengths and interests.

Since we derive so many benefits from play or having fun together, leaders need to give attention to it in their workplaces and see it as an essential element of creating a healthy workplace culture. Leaders often get caught up in the responsibilities of running an organization and getting the work done. But when that happens, having fun is easy to ignore, or it can become one more item on a busy agenda that the leader needs to check off their list. In my view, this is a mistake.

But here is a conundrum for leaders who want to make sure their staff have fun at work: having fun is not something that can be forced or mandated. When I am told by someone in power, like a manager, that we are going to get together for some office-mandated "fun" like a day of team-building activities, I find myself reluctant to take part. It feels as though I am being compelled to have fun – normal fun just isn't like that. When children play, it happens naturally as they interact with their environment and each other. When parents turn fun into an obligation by saying, "Play nice with that kid," it rarely leads to a fun time. And in my experience, adults aren't too different. Fun needs to happen naturally as a part of being together and not as something that

Instead of prescribing fun, I believe leaders need to make space for play to evolve organically and join in when they can.

people are told to do for a day of team building.

Instead of prescribing fun, I believe leaders need to make space for play to evolve organically and join in when they can. This does not mean that leaders should be totally hands off. Instead, there are several things a leader can do to encourage playfulness at work.

Leaders can start by introducing some elements into the environment that encourage playfulness. This can be as simple as having some squeeze toys, adult coloring books, and puzzles on the staff table. Or it can be as complex as building a space to facilitate people coming together in creative ways. In our office, we have opted for the former approach. What I have noticed is how people will pick up a squeeze ball and toss it back and forth while they talk, color a page over lunch, or laugh at the comics someone has clipped and put on their door. These simple things create opportunities for people to have fun when and how they want.

Leaders should also put some of their time into playing or creating enjoyable work experiences. Not only will this model to employees that it is okay to have fun, but it will also give the leader the other positive benefits of play, such as stress reduction. Putting time into play means occasionally joining in the fun and taking time to laugh with others. One way I do this is by paying attention to the office group chat on our internal messaging app and contributing to the silliness when I can.

When an organization puts resources like time and money into something, it speaks volumes to employees. For this reason, I think leaders should also use some of the organization's resources to create opportunities for fun. I don't mean they have to pay for expensive items or activities like flying employees to a retreat center in the mountains, but rather that they should make funds and/or time available for employee events. Events like the office holiday party, attending fundraisers, or buying a round of drinks after work all give people opportunities to connect in different ways and have fun together. When people connect outside of the office, the novelty of new environments helps them get to know each other in different ways. Be sure to involve employees in planning and leading events so they don't have the effect of becoming an obligation made by the leader.

Finally, leaders should not engage in fun or play simply because it will make the team more productive. Instead, we should have fun because it's a very human thing to do. It helps us feel connected, reduces our stress, and builds trust, all of which result in happier people. When people are happier, they will lead better lives, and better work will come as a result.

REFLECTION QUESTIONS

1. As you consider your job history, at which organization did you have the most fun? What were your relationships like at that job? How did having fun enhance your work?
2. What is your current organization's approach to play? How involved are employees and leaders in planning activities that make space for fun?

PRACTICAL APPLICATION

During the next week, keep track of how many times you see people having fun or engaging in play at work and notice the effect on staff. Make a list of ways that you could add opportunities for play or fun in your workplace. Then plan two ways you will either make more space for play or participate in the fun yourself.

ADDITIONAL RESOURCE

Joy, Inc.: How We Built a Workplace People Love by Richard Sheridan (Portfolio, 2013)

42

BE INSPIRING

BY WENDY LOEWEN

When my children were younger, they were on our local swim team and spent countless hours in the pool working to improve their skills. They watched clips of swimming stroke techniques and spoke enthusiastically about their team to anyone who would listen. The team's motto was "See it. Believe it. Achieve it."

It was fascinating to watch how the coaches lived this motto and inspired the team. They did this by sharing their own personal road to success in the pool and in life, encouraging team members to believe in their ability to improve, and celebrating every individual and team achievement. This experience and the team's motto continue to remind me why being an inspiring leader is important in creating engagement and fostering workplace satisfaction. Below are three key things I learned from my children's swim team that apply to being an inspirational leader in the workplace.

Inspiring Leaders Show the Way

My children came to understand what it takes to become a good swimmer by listening as their coaches shared their own experiences. They often spoke of how they had come to love swimming and why they were committed to the sport. They described getting up at the crack of dawn on Saturday mornings to drive hours to a faraway swim meet while their friends were sleeping in. The coaches prepared the kids for what they would encounter in each town – even going as far as describing the shape and temperature of each pool, and where the best place was to get ice cream after the meet.

Good leaders generously share their wisdom, knowledge, and experiences because they have gone before us. Part of being an inspirational leader is allowing others to benefit from the lessons we have learned along the way. As leaders we often have the advantage of having seen and been exposed to more of what the working world has to offer, whether that is more experience in our industry, familiarity with our organization's systems, closer connection to clients, or more knowledge of future organizational plans. When we share our knowledge and wisdom with our staff, we inspire them to see what it takes to be successful in our organization. Inspiring leaders tell us stories that excite us, stories that we can see ourselves in – they do this intentionally and often.

Over the years, I have seen Randy and Eric begin most meetings and staff events with an inspirational story from our organization's past, something significant they are working on, a vision for a new venture, or occasionally even something they are wrestling with. Staff have come to look forward to these stories because they help everyone feel like they are part of an organization that is continuing to evolve, and they can see themselves in the story.

Inspiring Leaders Push for More

From the sidelines of the swimming pool, I watched how the coaches encouraged my children to always aim for their "personal best." Team members were told repeatedly that they should strive to get a bit faster at every swim meet and were reminded to watch their swim times carefully so they could track their own improvement. The focus was always on individual improvement rather than beating the competition. After each swim meet, there was a debriefing session where they affirmed every team member who improved their time, even if it was only by a few seconds. During practices, the swimmers were also encouraged to push for more. Once they had mastered one technique they were encouraged to move to the next phase of their development. Sometimes this was to get faster, sometimes it was to perfect a technique, and other times it was to learn a new swim stroke.

Inspiring leaders help those around them stretch themselves to grow and experience the sense of accomplishment that comes with learning and improving. Someone recently asked me if being an inspirational leader was akin to being a cheerleader no matter how bad the score. I quickly replied that this is not what it's about. Rather than settling for mediocrity, being an inspirational leader is about taking our commitment to growth and improvement seriously. In our role as leaders, we need not just to cheer but to concretely provide support for our staff to grow and develop. This happens when we encourage others to set goals that stretch and build their capacity. We inspire others by spurring people to believe in themselves, tackle new challenges, and build their confidence as they work to improve. Inspirational leaders are clear that being a valued team member isn't about competing with each other. Rather, it is about constant and consistent improvement no matter how small the gain.

SURVEY QUOTE

An effective leader is someone who inspires and challenges their staff to excel in ways they didn't think or believe were possible in their work.

Inspiring Leaders Take Time to Celebrate

One of the things I always appreciated about my children's coaches was that they were intentional about celebrating both small and big wins. They informally celebrated small wins as they happened during practices. When a swimmer had been struggling to master a particular stroke and was successful, they would shout words of affirmation from the poolside. Other times they privately affirmed the swimmers, quietly taking the time to make each person feel special. They were also intentional about gathering the team together to note successes more formally. Lunches in the park after practices and evening barbecues to celebrate team accomplishments were a regular part of the summer swim season.

In our role as leaders, recognizing victories requires us to really pay attention and to take the time from the busyness and the demands of our work to note where something positive has occurred. In my experience, this is well worth the effort. Leaders who celebrate accomplishments send a message that good work is noticed and matters. One of my personal mentors early in my career told me that what grows is what we pay attention to, and I believe this to be true. If we want our staff to be successful, we should take the time to recognize when they have reached a goal or milestone. This reaffirms the behaviors that allowed for the accomplishment to occur in the first place and sets the stage for it to happen again.

In our organization, we celebrate in several ways. First, we offer small validations for individual successes, whether that be through a heartfelt email or short conversation to note a job well done. We also take time during our monthly staff meetings to have individuals share an interesting project they have completed so we can celebrate their contributions. Another way we pause to celebrate our organizational successes is our annual holiday party. We all gather to share an evening of food, reflection, and celebration of our work. We tell stories and share pictures that highlight some of the collective achievements from the past year. This builds a sense of collaboration as we all celebrate together. Inspirational leaders know that celebrating people's accomplishments not only feels good, but it also propels the work of the organization forward in positive ways.

Inspiring leaders share the wisdom and knowledge they have gained from their experiences and encourage others to grow and learn. They set the stage for people to push themselves to the edges of their capacity, and they know the importance of celebrating successes, which generates enthusiasm and inspires others to take action.

REFLECTION QUESTIONS

1. Who has inspired you on your leadership journey? What did they do or say that was inspirational? What is important for you to remember from these experiences?
2. What does it mean to you to be an inspiring leader? What will you do to inspire others to action?

PRACTICAL APPLICATION

Look for examples of your colleagues doing things that connect to your organization's values, vision, or mission. Notice how what they do impacts the people around them. Then, at your next staff meeting or in a newsletter, share one of those stories and how you were inspired by it. Notice the response of those who hear your story.

ADDITIONAL RESOURCE

The Inspiring Leader: Unlocking the Secrets of How Extraordinary Leaders Motivate by John Zenger, Joseph Folkman, and Scott Edinger (McGraw-Hill Education, 2009)

43
TAKE A BREAK

BY RANDY GRIESER

There's a long-held understanding amongst our staff that they should be "worried" when I'm away on vacation. The first time that new hires learn I'm taking a vacation, longer serving staff inform them to prepare for something big upon my return. Their words of warning are related to a pattern that has occurred time and again over the course of our history at ACHIEVE – that I am often known to return from a vacation having made a big decision or with a new, innovative idea. For example, the idea for ACHIEVE Centre for Leadership was born while I was on vacation in Key West, Florida. The idea to create ACHIEVE Publishing (the publisher of this book) was born while I was on a vacation in France. And the idea for this book was developed while I was laying on a beach.

Early on in my role at ACHIEVE, I observed a pattern in myself that has allowed me to carve out vacations at just the right time to benefit not just myself but the organization. I have realized that I can't be effective and work full time without slowing down several times a year. And I even know myself well enough to know the specific times of the year that I need to take a break.

The first of these times is in January – and almost always involves sitting in the sun on some beach, not doing much of anything other

A vacation or break from work should leave you refreshed, inspired, and ready to get back to work.

than reading books (truth be told, they are most often related to marketing, strategy, and business) or *The Economist* (as I only have enough time to read this lengthy magazine on vacation). I also always travel with a notepad to record my thoughts and ideas. The second of these times is June. After a big push from February to May, I am ready for a break right at the start of summer – July is too long for me to wait.

I see my vacations as crucial to my ability to lead our organization. For one, I return to work energized, excited, and focused – ready to tackle projects and goals. But most importantly, slowing down allows me time to *think*, particularly about big issues affecting our organization.

While I can often carve out moments of time during a regular work week, the reality is that, for larger items, there is rarely enough time for me to fully consider, analyze, and decide on an approach. Instead, I am too often running from one meeting, project, or deadline to the next and I put off taking the time I need to just *think* and consider some of the bigger issues impacting our organization.

This time to think is so important that if I am struggling with a decision and there's a vacation coming up, I will often put it off until then. For example, one of my most recent vacations provided the opportunity I needed to consider a staffing issue I had been struggling with for months. After taking a break, I returned with clarity about what needed to be done. I was ready to act decisively rather than put things off any longer or make the wrong decision.

You may be observing by now that my "vacations" don't really seem like vacations. Rather they are more like *working vacations*. The reality is that as the founder of ACHIEVE I have never been able – or even wanted – to fully shut off for more than a few days at a time. As a result, much of my vacation *is* filled with little moments of work-related activities. However, I do consider these slowed-down periods of vacation and work sufficient for me.

A vacation or break from work should leave you refreshed, inspired, and ready to get back to work. But the time needed to fully be away from working to feel refreshed will vary for each leader. Some leaders need more time than me, and some need less. My encouragement is that instead of focusing on the number of days away from work, try to take the time you need to feel refreshed, inspired, and ready to go back to work.

An important part of any leader's job should be to take enough time to think, relax, and refresh. Many of us are in leadership positions because we have demonstrated our ability to act, but that often comes at the expense of thinking. Taking the time to truly think and reflect on major decisions is crucial to our own and our organizations' continued growth. So, if you haven't done so in a while, take a break – it's good for you and your organization.

REFLECTION QUESTIONS

1. What is your attitude toward taking breaks from work? Do you allow and even embrace periods where you slow down and get time to think? How often, for how long, and at what times do you need time away from work to feel refreshed, inspired, and ready to get back to work?

2. What is your organization's attitude about taking breaks from work? What could you do to make sure you and others are taking appropriate breaks from work?

PRACTICAL APPLICATION

Think about your pattern of vacations and consider what is working well for you and what isn't. Based on what you observe, plan and, if needed, adjust your vacation plan for the year. After each vacation, make a note to consider how you feel afterward– did it make you feel refreshed, inspired, and ready to get back work? If not, readjust your plan.

ADDITIONAL RESOURCES

Time Off: A Practical Guide to Building Your Rest Ethic and Finding Success Without the Stress by John Fitch and Max Frenzel (Time Off LLC, 2020)

TED Talk: "The Power of Time Off" by Stefan Sagmeister

44

LEADING THROUGH CONFLICT

BY ERIC STUTZMAN

Early in my career, I worked as a mediator and saw firsthand how poorly managed conflict can impact a workplace. After years of simmering conflict, the owners of a welding business had finally decided to hire external mediators for some help. Many small, unresolved grievances had built up over time among the staff, and when someone had a complaint about another employee, the manager often ignored the situation or, in some cases, came down hard on the whole group for being "petty." These kinds of responses made staff reluctant to involve leadership in other issues, and the result was predictable. By the time I was called to help, some of the welders would no longer speak with one another and were even refusing to work the same shifts as other colleagues.

When it comes to managing conflict in the workplace, *how* leadership responds matters a great deal. Early on in my work with ACHIEVE, I worked with a difficult office-related conflict. It required me to give a fair amount of my leadership time to the issue for a couple of weeks. When the matter was resolved, I remember staff remarking that they appreciated that I took the issue seriously and acted with care.

An effective leader is comfortable addressing conflicts and responds to them immediately and respectfully.

As part of our research for our book, *The Culture Question*, we conducted a 2,400-person survey asking a series of questions related to workplace culture. First, we asked whether people agreed or disagreed that they had a great place to work. Then we asked them to respond to a series of survey statements, including several about conflict resolution. Some of what we discovered surprised us.

As expected, we saw a strong relationship between people liking where they work and the statement, "People in my workplace deal with conflict constructively." The surprise came when we asked for responses to, "Leaders in my organization work to resolve conflict quickly." This statement had an even stronger relationship with whether people said they liked their workplace. We also noticed that people who said they had an unhealthy workplace were much more likely to strongly disagree that their leaders dealt with conflict quickly. It seems clear that how leaders respond to conflict plays an important role in having a healthy workplace.

In my work as a mediator and consultant, I have paid close attention to the significant impact of leadership on conflict resolution. In addition to responding to conflict quickly, leaders must also handle it well or they will make it worse. I believe that most leaders can be effective at conflict management when they internalize and act on the following truths.

Take Conflict Seriously

As leaders, we often find out about conflict when someone confides in us or it erupts in a public manner, like at a meeting. When someone confides in you, remember that most people want to be able to deal with conflict on their own and only approach leadership when they feel stuck or need help. People usually don't make their conflicts public until they feel fed up. If you hear about conflict, take it seriously and be sure to act promptly.

Ignoring Tension Is a Choice

If your response to a conflict is inaction, it will be interpreted as meaning one of three things: for some it validates their behavior; others see it as a message that you don't care about the situation or don't want to provide leadership; and some will interpret your silence as a lack of competence. Don't let this happen, even if conflict scares you. Silence is one of the worst mistakes that leaders routinely make. It allows conflict to fester and grow, and it kills morale – so take action and do something about it.

How You Act Matters

Your actions should carry the message that you care – that you want to see a positive resolution to the tension or disagreement, and that you trust your people to act with good intentions. Those involved in the conflict should understand that you're there to make sure there is good process for resolving the conflict rather than to choose a side.

Avoid Fixing the Problem for Others

While you may need to play a role in the resolution of a conflict, the best solutions come from the people involved. When people act on their own solutions, they are more likely to be happy with the result. Your job is to create the environment where others are empowered to ask questions and come up with positive ways forward, and then support each person to follow through on what they said they would do.

Call For Values-Based Behavior

Help people draw on their best behavior by anchoring your conversation in their values and those of the organization. Remind people of their own positive intentions and the probable positive intentions of anyone else involved in the conflict. When people consider how they want to be in the world *and* how their organization wants them to act, it leads to proactive and pro-social behavior rather than the typical reactiveness in conflict.

Model What You Want

In most conflicts, what people ultimately want is to be understood. When they are heard, they will be more likely to move forward. As a leader you should demonstrate how to listen. Let people know what you hear them saying and ask if *they* have heard and understood what others involved in the conflict are saying. Help them think about how they can listen and encourage them to speak in ways that will increase their likelihood of being heard.

Also, demonstrate the importance of taking responsibility. You can do this by explaining to those involved in the conflict the ways you may have contributed to an environment where conflict is growing. Showing people how to listen and taking responsibility for your actions (or inaction) will encourage them to do the same.

Curiosity Will Bear More Fruit than Judgment

Perhaps the most important realization for any leader when it comes to leading through conflict is that they must lead themselves and others to listen and act with curiosity rather than judgment. In conflict, people begin to perceive the actions of other people through a negative lens, which leads to negative judgments about their character. When seen through the lens of conflict, previously innocent behavior like a suggestion for how to improve something may now be interpreted as criticism.

Our job as leaders is to hear the tension-filled stories of others, acknowledge their experiences, and then move them toward curiosity so that they will be open to listening and seeing the situation from the other's perspective. Once we have listened to someone, we can then begin helping them consider alternatives to explain the offending behavior that don't include negative intent or a character problem in the other person. When people are curious, they are more open to dialogue and can begin to seriously consider how to resolve the conflict.

It's Smart to Ask For Help

If you are feeling stuck or think the situation is beyond your skill level, don't be afraid to reach out to another leader, someone from human resources with expertise, or a mediator for assistance. This shows that you care and that you want to help your people. We all benefit from the skillful perspective and assistance others can provide. Sometimes even mediators utilize other mediators to work through conflict – I know I have.

As we discovered in our survey for *The Culture Question*, leadership's quick action in response to conflict is key to creating a great work environment. In addition, *how* leaders act makes a great deal of difference in shaping the outcome of any conflict, so rely on these simple truths to guide your actions.

REFLECTION QUESTIONS

1. Consider a time when you were involved in resolving a conflict. How could you have been more curious? What would you do differently next time?
2. As you consider your current workplace, what are you already doing well? Which of the truths listed in this insight needs more attention? Why?

PRACTICAL APPLICATION

Meet with the other leaders in your organization to discuss how you can be consistent when leading others through conflict. Together, consider how you can support people as they work through conflict, and determine who you can go to for help with the more difficult conflicts.

ADDITIONAL RESOURCES

"Practice Constructive Conflict Management" in *The Culture Question: How to Create a Workplace Where People Like to Work* by Randy Grieser, Eric Stutzman, Wendy Loewen, and Michael Labun (ACHIEVE Publishing, 2019)

The Good Fight: Use Productive Conflict to Get Your Team and Organization Back on Track by Liane Davey (Page Two Books, 2019)

45

TAKE A LOOK
IN THE MIRROR

BY WENDY LOEWEN

Like most organizations, at ACHIEVE we carefully choose the people we hire. We want employees who will make a substantial contribution, are committed to working collaboratively, and identify with our values. Part of our hiring process is to have a panel interview for prospective candidates. After each interview, the panel has a candid and open conversation about each person's strengths and weaknesses, how we think they will fit in with our team, and whether their personal values align with our organizational values.

After a recent set of interviews for a position at our office, I was telling my son about our process. He looked at me and asked, "Do you ever apply that same process for evaluating your own performance?" His question really struck me because I believe he was on to something important.

SURVEY QUOTE

A good leader is someone who is aware of their own weaknesses.

As leaders, we should also be applying the same expectations and critical evaluation we use in the hiring process to ourselves. With constant and pressing demands, it is not easy to pause for self-evaluation. But if we want to continue facing the challenges of our work, be passionate about what we are doing, and be able to contribute to our organization's success, it is crucial that we take the time to evaluate our own leadership.

If we apply the same filters that we use in our interview process, then part of our self-evaluation should include identifying our strengths, assessing our weaknesses, understanding where our strengths fit with our team, and reflecting on our values. I took up my son's challenge and used the following questions to guide my self-evaluation (they are adapted from our interview questions).

What Am I Good At?

Identifying what we are good at is crucial for us to be able to perform in our leadership role. One of my strengths is generating ideas. I derive a lot of satisfaction from creatively looking at how to deliver our content, and it is exciting for me to come up with new ways to meet our clients' needs. That said, I am also aware that it is easy for me to overlook my present commitments, and this can be problematic if I do not realistically assess the time and energy required to pursue a new idea.

Knowing my strengths and weaknesses helps me see where I should direct my energy and which tasks or activities might be best to delegate. I recently took an online strengths-based assessment that helped me understand what I am naturally good at. There are many assessment tools to help you consider your strengths, and a quick internet search will give you many options.

How Do My Leadership Strengths Fit with Those of My Team?

Part of evaluating our leadership should involve considering how our strengths complement those of our team. At ACHIEVE we have found it is important to take the time to individually reflect on our strengths – and then to gather as a leadership team to share our reflections. We use this time to seek feedback and help each other evaluate our leadership. These open conversations tell us who we can lean on for support and who has strengths in areas that are different from our own.

On our leadership team, I know that Randy is a logical thinker, and if I need help thinking through how to approach a big project, he can prioritize quickly and point out what I need to keep in mind. Eric can take the smallest idea and make it better. I know that when I am stuck on a project, he will be able to help me build off what I have already done or any idea that I bring to him, no matter how small. Understanding how our strengths fit with our team is motivating because it allows us to make the best use of our collective abilities, and ultimately to do the best work possible.

How Aligned Are My Personal Values with Those of My Organization?

Part of evaluating our leadership should occasionally include assessing our own values to ensure they are still in line with those of our organization. This has been a key part of my own journey as I have always sought to work for organizations that have values that align with my own. Growing up, my parents stressed the importance of congruence between a person's actions and their beliefs. My dad was a church minister and "Practice what you preach" was a common phrase in our home. My parents often reminded us that our actions needed to embody our beliefs and that our beliefs are meant to be lived out, not just spoken of.

Similarly, one of our core values at ACHIEVE is to *embody*, meaning we practice what we teach. We teach about respectful workplaces, so we hold each other accountable to act respectfully. We teach about the importance of curiosity in conflict resolution, so when we have conflict on our team, we remind each other to be curious. This value of embodying what we teach is central to the work we do and is aligned with my personal values. In addition, when we are clear about our values, they can act as a reference point to ensure that the decisions we make and the actions we take are congruent with both our personal and organizational values. To know that I work with an organization that allows me to express and live out my values is inspiring.

Just like we evaluate the anticipated contributions of new hires, we should take the time to evaluate our own leadership. This self-evaluation should be an ongoing process so that we can continually improve and develop our leadership skills. Taking time to evaluate our leadership allows us to move forward with the knowledge that we are contributing our best strengths to our teams and giving our organization the best shot at succeeding.

REFLECTION QUESTIONS

1. Have you ever felt that your personal values conflicted with an organization where you worked? What was the impact of that? Consider a time when you felt your values aligned with your workplace. How did that impact you differently?
2. What unique skill sets do you possess that make you an asset to your team? How are you currently drawing on your strengths and values at work? How will you continue to evaluate your leadership?

PRACTICAL APPLICATION

Take some time to reflect on your strengths (you might want to do an online assessment as a part of this process). Consider what you do in your leadership role and how your organization might suffer if it were not for your work. Write these reflections and discoveries down and come back to them over time. Invite the members of your leadership team to consider doing the same and ask them if they would be willing to share their reflections.

ADDITIONAL RESOURCE

Strengths-Based Leadership: Great Leaders, Teams, and Why People Follow by Barry Conchie and Tom Rath (Gallup Press, 2009)

46

WHAT WILL HAPPEN WHEN YOU'RE NOT THERE?

BY RANDY GRIESER

In addition to trying new foods, the thing I like most about traveling through Europe is seeing all the old buildings and bridges. When my family and I visit a new area, we quickly assess and figure out a plan to see as many "old" things as we can. To see structures with stone foundations that are hundreds, sometimes thousands of years old is truly remarkable. They were built with longevity in mind, from materials and with designs that have withstood the test of time.

In addition to studying European architecture, I'm equally fascinated with companies that have been around for a long time. This includes businesses like JPMorgan Chase & Co. (founded in 1799) and HarperCollins (founded in 1817), but I am equally if not more intrigued by the longevity of small- to medium-sized businesses, like my friend's family farm that is now owned and operated by their fourth generation, or my local lumber store now run by the fifth generation of the family.

If you look at businesses throughout history and analyze the research, you'll soon realize that these companies are the exception, not the norm. About 80 percent of new businesses survive more than two years, but by five years only 55 percent survive. And by the 15-year mark, only 25 percent of businesses remain.[1] The trajectory continues

– the more time that goes by, the less likely it is for a business to remain operational. Most research in the area of longevity is focused on businesses, so the same statistics may not apply to all sectors. However, I believe that most organizations do have a limited shelf life.

I've been thinking a lot about the longevity of ACHIEVE, the organization I founded. This is partially because I am at a transitional stage in life – my last child is graduating from high school, my wife and I are moving, and although I'm still involved and working at ACHIEVE, I recently stepped back from my role as CEO. All of this has culminated in me pondering more deeply about what's next for ACHIEVE – what do the next 15 or even 50 years look like? What do we do today to position ourselves to still be providing valuable services and products well into the future?

Many of the things already reviewed in this book provide a solid foundation for longevity. In other words, we need to keep doing the things that have made us successful. For example, visioning for the future and fostering innovation are crucial parts of the foundation of longevity. Another of the main layers to this foundation is *culture*. Cultures, whether they're healthy or toxic, tend to become solidified over time. And organizations with healthy cultures will be able to weather whatever challenges come their way.

Another main part of the foundation is *people* – both leaders and staff. When we bring new people into the organization, it is vital to pay close attention to how and who we hire. In doing so, we work to solidify our foundation for the future. Bringing the wrong people into the organization can have dire consequences, and this is particularly true when it comes to leadership. The continuity and congruency of good leadership within an organization is critical for its survival.

Unfortunately, I have observed that too many organizations don't intentionally work to develop leaders or think about succession planning until it's too late. While our research found that the majority of organizations do provide opportunities and pay for leadership development, the emphasis is on experienced leaders.

SURVEY STATISTICS

Of the respondents who reported that their organization provides opportunities for them to develop as a leader, 64 percent also said that their organization pays for their leadership development.

Here is the percentage of leaders and their years of experience who reported that their organization pays for leadership development activities:

- **58%** of leaders with 0–5 years' experience
- **64%** of leaders with 6–20 years' experience
- **72%** of leaders with 20+ years' experience

Interestingly, organizations are more likely to pay for leadership development for experienced leaders than for new leaders.

Far too often I have seen an organization struggle for years and sometimes disappear because the founder or long-term leader leaves with short notice – sometimes at no fault of their own – and only once the resignation is received does the organization begin to think about succession planning. If this scenario is combined with a lack of internal leadership development, meaning there isn't a good, qualified candidate from within the organization, organizations are forced to make snap decisions and hire externally. Sometimes the stars align and, despite the need to move quickly, a great candidate is found, but too often the opposite happens.

Given the significant role leadership plays in an organization's longevity, lack of planning for leadership development and succession planning is a critical error. One wrong CEO or executive director could mean the difference between surviving or not.

To counter this risk, I believe strongly that current leaders should be talking about leadership development and succession planning at

One of our jobs as leaders is to prepare the next generation of leaders.

least several times a year. One of our jobs as leaders is to prepare the next generation of leaders, so we should be intentional about identifying, coaching, and encouraging leadership development at all levels within our workplace.

When it comes to the highest levels of leadership, it can be helpful to take a five- to 10-year view into the future. In our own personal experience, the planning for our senior leadership transition began years in advance. And even though we have just made the transition, we continue to think about succession planning. Given that we anticipate Eric (my successor) has many years ahead of him at our organization, this is not detailed planning, but we are still considering potential candidates both internally and externally for high-level leadership – and we're planning for what we need to do to develop them. *For more on this topic, read When Leadership Transitions on page 154.*

Organizations that last and stand the test of time know how crucial good leadership is, and they don't wait and hope for the best. Rather, they focus on enhancing and growing leaders for succession well in advance. The good news is that these efforts pay off not just for the future but in the present as well, because the leaders you are developing for tomorrow will also help you be a stronger organization today.

REFLECTION QUESTIONS

1. Which of your current staff have leadership potential? What have you done to build on that potential? What steps can you take now to further develop their potential?
2. What do you foresee the leadership needs of your organization to be in three, five, or 10 years from now? What can you do now to prepare for your future needs?

PRACTICAL APPLICATION

In the next month, gather your leadership team to talk about the future of your organization. Consider what you can do now to lay the foundation for longevity. Focus your discussion and planning not only on leadership development, but also on culture, vision, and innovation.

ADDITIONAL RESOURCE

Who Comes Next? Leadership Succession Planning Made Easy by Mary C. Kelly and Meridith E. Powell (Productive Leaders, 2020)

47

TAKING THE MYSTERY OUT OF INNOVATION

BY ERIC STUTZMAN

A few years ago, while working for a different organization, I learned firsthand about the wrong way to encourage innovation. While the organization did good work, we rarely had intentional conversations about how we could improve or create new services that our clients would value. In the absence of intentional innovation conversations, staff were left to figure out how to innovate on their own. To make matters worse, our innovative ideas were not always welcome.

After a conversation with a colleague in which we both expressed frustration around an area of inefficiency, I came up with an idea about creating a system that would allow us to work together more efficiently. When I went to my boss and presented her with a plan for how we could work together and create a better system, her response shocked me: "Eric, you've stepped out of line here – you should have consulted with me first before working on this." As a result of her reaction, I felt shut down, misunderstood, and unappreciated for my effort to make our work better. My ability to innovate and feel engaged plummeted.

I have often seen how organizations that do not innovate well tend to stagnate. Given our rapidly changing world, all leaders should focus on creating an atmosphere that encourages innovation. Innovation ensures that organizations remain relevant.

To create an innovative workplace, leaders need to understand what innovation is. I used to picture innovation as a vaguely mysterious process where highly intelligent people would cluster in front of a huge whiteboard filled with unfathomable equations, with the goal of reaching one of those elusive "eureka" moments. But after working at a highly innovative organization, I have learned that innovation involves everyone in purposeful processes that bring together ideas for solving problems. It is nurtured through creating an environment where people can experiment, share ideas, fail, and learn.

While there are many different definitions of innovation, I like to think of it as the act of *implementing* creative ideas for solving problems. Not every innovative idea is big – in fact, most are not. However, when combined, smaller innovations can make a substantial impact for our staff and the people we serve. Minor innovations include things like a simplified process for making a product, moving from hard copy to digital files, or the removal of an extra step in a form. Less common will be major innovations that change the way we provide services or offer a product in a significant way. Major innovations include items like new programs or product lines that require a lot of time, energy, and capital to implement.

In my own experience leading organizations, I have learned that how leaders approach new ideas and build systems for innovation significantly impacts engagement, workplace culture, and organizational outcomes. Leaders can start to create an innovative culture by nurturing an environment that welcomes ideas when inspiration strikes. But equally if not more important is that leaders provide structure that intentionally invites or plans for innovation. When they do, they significantly increase their odds for being a highly innovative organization.

Over the past number of years, the leadership team at ACHIEVE has worked diligently to create an environment that both encourages innovation and systematizes it so that we can harness its power. In addition to creating an environment that organically welcomes new ideas, we intentionally schedule an innovation day every year.

One of our most helpful discoveries is that we can take some of the mystery out of innovation by thinking about it as problem solving.

On that day, all staff stop their regular duties to focus on innovation. Each person is assigned to a team that combines big-picture thinkers, detail-oriented people, and those who excel in creating action plans. Then we ask a series of questions that each team must answer. As they generate and filter ideas, they write detailed minutes identifying who will do what by when. When the teams have finished meeting, we all gather to hear about the projects we have created and the time frames we have set for getting the work done. I then check in with the innovation project teams each month to see how they are progressing. This meeting typically generates enough projects to last six months to a year. It is highly energizing and motivating.

When our staff met for our innovation planning day this past year, we generated 66 innovation projects that we committed to pursuing. These projects ranged from small fixes to our systems that took only 30 minutes to complete, to big-picture changes to how we offer our materials that took many hours and (for some) months to complete. In reviewing the minutes about six months later, we had completed 63 of our projects. Only three remained on the list, and each of them was well on its way to being finished. This approach to innovation is exhilarating. It adds variety and interest to what we are doing. We make progress, we see how our ideas and efforts change things for the better, and our work is more meaningful as a result.

One of our most helpful discoveries is that we can take some of the mystery out of innovation by thinking about it as problem solving. When you consider innovation as a problem-solving process, you can quickly zero in on some key questions that will guide your discussion.

We like to use the following two questions to help focus our innovation discussions:

- **What's bugging you?** This question gets people thinking about daily and weekly irritations that they would like to fix. We have found that it is incredibly satisfying to fix something that has created ongoing irritation. We have fixed everything from a poor filing system to squeaky doors to website issues.
- **What are some common problems that our clients have and how can we fix them?** This question gets us to take the perspective of the people we serve. It can either be asked as a general question or in relation to the services we provide. Either way, this turns our focus to how we can provide more helpful and relevant services to the people we serve.

Of course, some innovations will fail. As my co-author Randy writes in his book, *The Ordinary Leader*, "One of the most important aspects of establishing an innovative organizational culture is embracing failure as a part of innovation. All innovation involves the possibility of failure. Trying something and failing should be viewed as a learning experience and a part of the process."[1] We have learned that failure is okay and that we might just find some gold as a result. Instead of asking who or what we can blame, we ask *what we can learn.* Failure not only teaches us what not to do – it can also lead us to other discoveries that we did not anticipate.

Innovation should not be viewed as a mysterious or abstract process; instead, leaders should focus on creating an environment that welcomes ideas, and they should plan for innovation to happen. As we generate new ideas, solve problems, and learn from our failures, our successes will propel us to new and better work.

REFLECTION QUESTIONS

1. As you consider your work history, have there been times when your good ideas were shut down? What was the result for you and your organization? What could have been done differently?
2. In what ways is your organization innovative? What factors might be affecting people's ability to be innovative? How do people treat failure as it relates to innovation? How is innovation encouraged?

PRACTICAL APPLICATION

Schedule a half or full day to sit down with other leaders for the purpose of creating an innovation plan. To help get you started, download and print our "Focused Innovation" handout by visiting the Free Resources section of our website (www.achievecentre.com). Ask each person to answer the questions on this worksheet in advance. Then, at your meeting, share your ideas and make commitments to innovation projects.

ADDITIONAL RESOURCES

"Creativity and Innovation" in *The Ordinary Leader: 10 Key Insights for Building and Leading a Thriving Organization* by Randy Grieser (ACHIEVE Publishing, 2017)

TED Talk: "The Surprising Habits of Original Thinkers" by Adam Grant

48

IS IT TIME TO TERMINATE PERFORMANCE REVIEWS?

BY WENDY LOEWEN

In a recent coaching session, the manager I was meeting with shared that she was procrastinating facilitating her staff's annual performance reviews. She explained how she tends to put off giving the reviews until the very last minute. As a result, she scrambles to prepare, spends a few sleepless nights worrying about how the reviews will go, and then "powers through" all of them in one jam-packed day. She concluded her assessment of performance reviews saying that she didn't really know what the point of them was other than to waste time and put everyone on her team, including herself, on edge.

It's no secret that employees also dislike performance reviews. Almost everyone I've talked to remembers a performance review that had a negative impact on them, causing a range of adverse emotions from anger and frustration to anxiety and sadness. This typically happens when managers use the review as an opportunity to run through a list of all the things a person has done wrong in the past year.

It's not difficult to see why this type of stand-alone yearly assessment is a problem. The focus on the past causes defensiveness and does little to set the stage for positive performance in the future. This kind of review is counterproductive because the behavior has already occurred, and the person is only hearing that they have done something problematic well after the fact. In a summary of the research on performance reviews, *The Washington Post* found that when constructive criticism is given, even employees who are keen to grow in their role are significantly bothered when they receive negative feedback.[1]

SURVEY QUOTE

A great leader is able to draw out strengths from employees and work with them to improve their skills to be more efficient and grow within an organization.

At ACHIEVE, we believe that providing ongoing connection through regular conversations in the context of our work is the best tool to promote performance, not an annual performance review. We also believe that the objective of performance management is to align the actions of the employee with the goals of the organization. This means we focus on performance *enhancement* and *growth*, not performance *reviews*. We have found that having regular check-ins, allowing staff to set their own goals, and focusing on building capacity are effective ways to manage performance. Each of these ideas will provide you with ways to enhance performance *without* facilitating the traditional performance review.

Schedule Frequent Check-Ins

Regular check-ins are a great way to increase engagement, workplace satisfaction, and performance. It has been my experience that people feel valued and affirmed when we pay attention to them, give them our time, and offer our support – and this should be the primary focus of our check-ins. These conversations should happen regularly and be a time where we ask what the person's priorities are, and what they need from us to be successful. Our role in managing performance should be to support staff, and then keep them accountable to reach their goals. When a person is engaging in behaviors that are not contributing to their success or to their team's productivity, they may need to hear from us about what isn't working and what needs to change. We can do this by presenting the impact of their actions, sharing our perspective on the situation, and asking what they believe needs to be done differently going forward.

When we share how someone's actions have impacted us or others, it creates opportunities for them to gain insight into what's working and what isn't. Frequent check-ins allow for timely conversations about issues that matter, and the result is that the person knows what to work on so they can improve their performance.

Invite Staff to Set Goals and Monitor Their Progress

One of the ways we can support our staff in being accountable for their own performance is to formally invite them to give us updates on what they are doing, where they are at with particular tasks and recent successes, or what they are struggling with. This is called *self-reporting* and it informs us of the staff's contribution to organizational goals that we might not have been aware of otherwise. It reinforces the fact that their contribution is of value and that their voice is important. When staff share their progress with us, we should be attentive, acknowledge their growth, and validate their efforts. This type of self-monitoring has the added benefit of making staff more conscious of how they are contributing.

At ACHIEVE, we also take time to listen to our employee's goals for the future in an annual goal-setting meeting. This conversation follows an agenda that includes reflection questions about how their work is going and what their objectives are for the coming year. Once priorities are outlined, we have a conversation and ask them to identify their best course of action. This is important because we know that people learn and perform best when they take personal responsibility for their actions. In addition to the practice of providing ongoing feedback, our goal-setting meeting has replaced traditional performance reviews.

Focus On Building Capacity

Helping someone get better at their job is a large part of a leader's role. To build capacity in our employees, we need to inspire and motivate them to be active participants in their own development. We can do this by identifying and affirming the strengths of our employees.

Years ago, we hired a person for a client services role, but it quickly became apparent that she had skill in graphic design. With time and opportunity, she continued to build her skills and significantly contributed to our organization in this regard. Opportunities like this are why we need to be attentive and build on the strengths our employees bring to the table. Rather than investing too much time in trying to fix skill deficits, choose to put energy, resources, and time into helping people discover and capitalize on their unique strengths and contributions.

Performance management should always be about growth and development, and this cannot occur in an annual or even intermittent performance review that focuses only on problem areas. Rather, we need to make an ongoing commitment to improving performance by using strategies like the ones listed above. Though these strategies take time and effort to implement, they provide multiple perspectives on performance and a more well-rounded picture of how the employee is doing than a traditional review. This is because they highlight areas for improvement *and* provide ongoing opportunities for development based on strengths. Organizations that focus on finding ways to support their staff to grow and develop will have better results – and this should be the goal of any performance-management plan.

REFLECTION QUESTIONS

1. What has been your experience with performance reviews? Consider what it's like to be on the receiving end of a performance review and consider your experience in delivering them. What have you found helpful? What hasn't been helpful? What have you learned?
2. In what ways are you supporting your staff to improve their performance? How often and in what ways do you check in with your staff? How are you inviting staff to be responsible for their own performance? What more could you do?

PRACTICAL APPLICATION

Schedule a time to meet with each of your staff. Let them know that you would like to continue to meet with them regularly to hear about their priorities and how you can be a support to them. Ask them what kind of feedback they find meaningful and helpful. Make a plan to check in with them on a regular basis that works for you both.

ADDITIONAL RESOURCE

Next Generation Performance Management: The Triumph of Science Over Myth and Superstition by Alan L. Colquitt (Information Age Publishing, 2017)

49

WHAT'S YOUR PHILOSOPHY OF LEADERSHIP?

BY RANDY GRIESER

"What is your philosophy of leadership?" To some people this question can be daunting and difficult to answer. In fact, I was sometimes met with a blank, deer-in-the-headlights stare when I asked leaders about this during interviews I conducted for my first book, *The Ordinary Leader.* I found it surprising that so many people had not taken the time to fully develop their thoughts about what it means to be a leader.

One of the reasons it's so important to have a philosophy of leadership is because of what we found in the survey conducted for this book: A leader's confidence in their own leadership abilities is related to having a clear philosophy of leadership. Ninety percent of those who reported they have a clear philosophy of leadership feel confident in their leadership abilities, as opposed to 32 percent of those who do not have a clear philosophy of leadership.

How do you articulate your leadership philosophy? In my experience, there is a spectrum of leadership philosophies that usually falls somewhere between *relational* and *authoritarian.* Relational leaders trust employees to make meaningful contributions, while authoritarian leaders outline the consequences of not meeting expectations. Relational leadership is about *enabling* success, while authoritarian leadership is about *demanding* success.

Relational leaders build relationships with employees and promote collaborative decision-making, information sharing, and teamwork. They assume the best in employees and use influence built on trust and relationships to motivate. Authoritarian leaders use positional power to actively structure the work of employees and lay out expectations for compliance. They assume the worst in employees and use threats and punishments to motivate.

The key element of relational leadership is *trust*. These leaders have earned trust and are therefore able to influence others without using coercion. When you care about your employees and have *their* interests in mind – not just the organization's – you increase your influence with them. However, this does not mean that relational leaders should never be directive in their approach. Sometimes there are circumstances when a relational leader needs to be directive, like when someone is clearly doing something that will cause harm. You can still be a relational leader but be directive when the circumstances require a directive approach. The key reason this can still work without damaging the relationship is because the directive action is rooted in the trust built by a philosophy of relational leadership. In this way, the *action* of being directive is different than the philosophy of being authoritarian.

By now it should be clear that my philosophy of leadership is on the relational end of the spectrum. I say "end of the spectrum" because there are leaders, even within my own organization, who are more relational than me. Due to a variety of reasons including personality traits and experience, some people will be more relational than others. But I make no apologies that I believe all leaders should embrace a philosophy that emphasizes the importance of relationships. When we

Relational leadership is about enabling success, while authoritarian leadership is about demanding success.

get to know our employees on a human level – when we *care* about our employees – we build trust. And with trust, employees will move mountains *with* you rather than *for* you.

Congruency of Leadership Across the Organization

In my consulting work, one of the most common issues I find within medium to large organizations is inconsistency in how different managers "do" leadership. Instead of having a crystal-clear vision and approach for how the organization views and lives out leadership, there is often a patchwork of philosophies and approaches. This typically results in confusion and, at worst, disengaged and disgruntled employees.

Time and again, I have seen organizations place limits on their success and growth by allowing leaders to have different leadership philosophies. When one manager is relational and caring while another is authoritarian and indifferent, you can rest assured that, over time, the organization will not perform at its peak. I believe that a unified philosophy of leadership on the relational side of the spectrum is crucial to long-term organizational success.

To build congruency in leadership philosophies, focus on these four elements:

- Write down your organization's leadership philosophy. This helps you remain accountable to it and aids in orienting new leaders.
- Regularly communicate your philosophy. This will assist your leadership team in being accountable to the philosophy and consistent in applying it.
- When hiring or promoting leaders, assess their leadership philosophy for congruency with the organization's. This will help you maintain congruency on your leadership team.
- Discuss management issues through the lens of your philosophy. This will ensure you apply your philosophy of leadership to everyday situations.

If you look around your organization and see different philosophies of leadership, I encourage you to talk about it. Have open conversations in an effort to clarify and agree on your organization's approach to leadership and seek ways to bring about greater alignment with it. Starting from when you hire new leaders, discuss your philosophy and incorporate it regularly into your leadership discussions.

SURVEY STATISTICS

While it is fairly common for leaders to have their own clear philosophy of leadership, it is much less likely that their personal philosophy lines up with the philosophies of other leaders at their organization. Whereas 71 percent of respondents agreed with the statement, "I have a clear philosophy of leadership," only 38 percent agreed with the statement, "My organization's leaders have a congruent philosophy of leadership."

Of respondents who felt their organization has a congruent leadership philosophy, 75 percent also reported high levels of trust between leadership and staff, as opposed to 10 percent of respondents who said there is not a congruent leadership philosophy.

Respondents who work for social service organizations reported the highest rates of a congruent leadership philosophy. Of those who reported that leaders at their organizations have a congruent philosophy of leadership:

- **43%** are in social services
- **37%** are in education
- **33%** are in healthcare
- **32%** are in government
- **29%** are in business

When we are intentional about articulating our leadership philosophy at an individual *and* an organizational level, we are more accountable to living it out. When we are faced with difficult leadership decisions, having a clear leadership philosophy makes it easier to determine how to make consistent decisions that support the work of the organization and create trust with our staff.

REFLECTION QUESTIONS

1. What kind of leader are you? Is your leadership philosophy more authoritarian or relational? What are the impacts of using this philosophy?
2. Do leaders in your workplace (all leaders, not just executive) practice a philosophy of leadership that is congruent with each other? If not, what could be done to create greater congruency?

PRACTICAL APPLICATION

This week, ask a variety of leaders, both within your organization and outside of it, "What is your philosophy of leadership?" In addition, suggest that your leadership team meet to discuss your organizational leadership philosophy.

ADDITIONAL RESOURCE

The Art of Caring Leadership: How Leading with Heart Uplifts Teams and Organizations by Heather R. Younger (Berrett-Koehler Publishers, 2021)

50

BUILDING A GREAT TEAM

BY ERIC STUTZMAN

Over the past few years, I have come to appreciate the value of connected and healthy teams in the workplace. This became especially clear to me when we successfully planned and ran our first major conference. Conferences require vision, data management, marketing, speaker coordination, coaching, customer service, and so much more. It takes a whole team of talented people who communicate well to pull it off. However, after months of planning, we had to cancel the in-person conference at the last minute and move it online. Despite the setback, our conference team kept their heads up, continued communicating, and were able to pull off a remarkable event. So, what makes something like this possible?

A team is a group of people who work interdependently toward a common purpose. The strength of our teams forms the basis for our performance as individuals and as an organization. Human beings are wired for connection, and teams are a vital part of that connection in the workplace. Through our relationships, our collective intelligence makes it possible for us to succeed and thrive. Yet relationships and teams need to be tended like a garden. With the right seeds, good things can grow, but we need to be vigilant about "feeding" and "weeding" to keep our teams healthy.

Human beings are wired for connection, and teams are a vital part of that connection in the workplace.

Based on my experience, there are five principles for building and maintaining a great team.

Select the Right People

As author Jim Collins famously articulated in his book *Good to Great*, we need to make sure we get "the right people on the bus."[1] In other words, team selection should not be accidental. Building a strong team means paying attention during the hiring process and focusing on bringing in the right people who will complement existing strengths and add diversity of thought to the team. Having diversity in talent also enhances the team's capabilities and collective intelligence.

Leaders need to be involved in the hiring processes. Their role is to determine the talents a new hire needs in order to add to the team's existing skill set. Leaders also need to look for someone who will bring a unique perspective to the team as that will strengthen their overall capabilities.

Learn How to Work Together

A collection of people working in the same department is not really a team unless they share common goals and work together to achieve them. Collaborating on projects allows team members to benefit from their collective intelligence, which boosts the quality and effectiveness of their projects beyond anything any one of them could have accomplished on their own.

Leaders should ensure that their teams have projects to work on together and that they have created clarity about how each person is interdependent on the others. As teams begin to achieve their goals, celebrate the ways in which they have relied upon each other and notice their shared accomplishments. This will help strengthen relationships and reinforce the value of the team.

Know and Draw On Each Other's Strengths

Working together creates an environment where team members can get to know everyone's strengths and learn how to rely on each other. Additionally, we have found that using simple personality assessment tools* can help people develop self-awareness, as well as an appreciation for each other's strengths.

A leader's role is to ask each team member how they can contribute to the group through their strengths and to get them thinking about how they benefit from the strengths of others. This can be done through simple questions like, "What can you contribute to this team effort?" or statements of appreciation such as, "I can see how each of you brings something unique to the group that is making us all stronger."

Involve and Listen to Every Voice

All too often I have heard people complain that they are not listened to in their place of work, and that they feel shut down when they contribute an idea or offer a suggestion. This is unfortunate because we hire people with the belief that they will bring something unique and valuable to the team. We hire people because they have brains and can think, so we must engage their minds. This means intentionally giving space for people to contribute to consultation processes and decisions. It means asking staff to engage and be mindful of their work processes and involving them in problem-solving and innovation. When we do this, we communicate that everyone is valuable, and it primes the pump for teams to benefit from their collective wisdom and experience.

The leader's job is to include voices and to listen. When you realize

---

* Two good assessment tools you can use are the CliftonStrengths assessment or the ACHIEVE Work Styles assessment.

that you do not have the corner on knowledge and wisdom as a leader (nor do you need to), you will naturally start to ask for contributions from others on your team. And when you engage their brains and listen to what they have to say, you will boost involvement and engagement.

Show That You Care

One of the things the world continues to teach us is that the human experience involves joy *and* struggle. We have likely all felt the pain of disconnection from loved ones and even from our colleagues at different times in our lives. We have seen how we need each other in ways that go beyond the function of our daily jobs. Our work teams need time to connect with each other as human beings and show each other care. Showing care strengthens relationships.

The leader's job is to make room for people to connect with each other beyond their work roles. This can be done through encouraging connections through events such as group coffee breaks, potlucks, or participating in a charity event such as a walk or gala.

It is within our power to create great teams, and it is worth the effort. There is something incredibly satisfying about pulling together in the same direction and achieving a result that could not have been done by one person. As it happens, these team results are also crucial for any organization that wants to survive and thrive. We need our teams to know how to work together, to depend on each other's strengths, and to be healthy enough to face crises as they arise. Let's all make building great teams one of our top priorities.

REFLECTION QUESTIONS

1. As you think about a recent team success, consider which of the principles listed above were the strongest contributors to that success. How did they contribute? Were any missing?
2. How can you create more time for attending to the strength of your team? What do you need to do as a leader to help your team grow stronger? What are you doing to build connections?

PRACTICAL APPLICATION

By the end of the month, have your team(s) participate in a personality assessment together. Or, if you have done one in the past year, revisit the outcomes with each other through an intentional conversation. This will help your teams get to know each other and improve your knowledge of team strengths while revealing areas where they could use some added diversity.

ADDITIONAL RESOURCES

"Create Peak Performing Teams" in *The Culture Question: How to Create a Workplace Where People Like to Work* by Randy Grieser, Eric Stutzman, Wendy Loewen, and Michael Labun (ACHIEVE Publishing, 2019)

High-Impact Tools for Teams: 5 Tools to Align Team Members, Build Trust, and Get Results Fast by Stefano Mastrogiacomo and Alexander Osterwalder (Wiley, 2021)

51
WHY YOUR VIBE MATTERS

BY WENDY LOEWEN

I was once asked to coach an employee whose manager said that he was "underperforming." In our first coaching session, the employee explained that he had a feeling of dread each morning about 20 seconds after his alarm rang. The feeling would arrive just as he realized that beginning another day meant having to go to work. He went on to say that his manager was grumpy most days and downright angry on the others. As a result, when the employee was at work, he would hide out in his office. This employee knew he was not meeting his potential, but he simply couldn't muster the emotional energy to do more than make it through the day. I left that coaching session saddened and reminded of the powerful effect our emotional reactions can have on others. It made me reflect on the impact my emotional tone can have on those I work with.

Whether or not we're aware of it, we are affected by the emotions of those around us. And when we are in a leadership position, our emotions and their effects are amplified. We should be mindful that our emotional responses (our "vibe") have a profound impact on the productivity and sense of personal well-being of those we supervise and work alongside. There is significant research demonstrating that emotions influence memory, perception, and cognition, all of which directly affect our ability to perform at work.[1] A leader's emotional reactions significantly influence how employees feel, which then impacts how motivated they are to tackle the challenges of their work.

This is exactly what happened in the case of the grumpy manager and the "underperforming" employee. Rather than supporting and encouraging good work, this manager did the opposite – and then *blamed* the employee rather than examining his own emotional tone. The employee in this session also told me that he was going home at the end of the day exhausted and in need of time to decompress. He explained that his partner also felt the effects of his manager's emotional reactions when he came home tired and emotionally drained; the negative emotions he felt at work were transferring beyond the workplace. This painful story illustrates a crucial point: a leader's emotions, whether they are negative or positive, have a ripple effect that reaches far beyond productivity.

Recently I arrived at work early because I knew my day was jam-packed with client calls, meetings, and ongoing projects. And for a variety of reasons, I was not in as good a mood as I normally am. However, when I got to the office, there was a buzz of positive activity and heartfelt greetings. As I walked to the kitchen to put my lunch in the refrigerator, I was greeted by one employee who was emptying the dishwasher while another was making herself a cup of coffee. From the moment I walked in the room, I recognized that I had a choice to make. I could frown, comment on the pressing work that needed to get done that day, dampen the mood, and prompt people to scamper off to their desks. Or, I could reinforce the positive emotions that were already in place.

Although I really didn't need another cup of coffee, I decided that this morning justified a second cup in order to join the conversation for a few minutes. The result was a quick check-in with what was going on in people's personal lives as well as what they were planning for their day. We all left energized, with half-finished cups of coffee and a reminder that we're part of a cohesive, productive team.

Our office is not perfect, but we are intentional about creating a healthy and positive workplace. I *feel* this every day when I walk in the door. I also recognize that, as a leader, I have a significant role to play in both creating and maintaining this positive emotional tone. While I am fortunate to have a great work environment, my consulting work has shown me that many organizations would be more productive and happier places to work if their leaders were aware of their own emotional reactions.

Whether we are catching or passing along emotions, leaders play a pivotal role in curating our environments for either the good or the bad. One of the most important ways to mitigate the potential harmful impacts of our negative emotions on others is simply by being aware that our emotions *are* influencing others. This awareness should then cause us to step back, evaluate, and regulate our emotions so that the way we express them at work each day is not harmful to those around us.

If our mood is not helpful or useful in supporting those we are leading, we need to change it! We are responsible for the emotions and attitudes we bring to our workplaces. When we find ourselves in a negative emotional state, we should take a moment to breathe and reduce our stress levels, and even avoid certain situations until we are able to respond in a manner that is helpful, kind, and positive. And remember, we can also make a difference in our workplaces by spreading positive emotions. If we are in a good mood, we shouldn't be afraid to smile more, speak about what is making us happy, and spread positive emotions.

REFLECTION QUESTIONS

1. Are there situations or individuals that regularly evoke a negative emotional response in you? If so, what do you think is the impact of your emotional responses?
2. How could you be more intentional about paying attention to your mood on a daily basis? How will you contribute to a positive emotional tone in your workplace?

PRACTICAL APPLICATION

Make it a priority to pay attention to your emotional responses this week. Keep a mood journal, and at the beginning and end of each workday note your mood, and what is contributing to it, and then make a choice about what you want to focus on. Take note of those situations in which you find it easy to respond calmly and with a positive tone, as well as those in which it is difficult. Look for patterns and themes that emerge. Identify the times where you tend to have negative emotional responses and make a plan for how to change these interaction patterns.

ADDITIONAL RESOURCE

Working with Emotional Intelligence by Daniel Goleman (Bantam Books, 2000)

52

LEADING IN
UNCERTAIN TIMES

BY ERIC STUTZMAN

The COVID-19 pandemic has provided useful insights about the effect leadership has on an organization's ability to handle challenging situations. In my consulting work, I have noticed stark differences in the ways leaders have responded to the challenges of the pandemic. In one instance, the executive director of an organization essentially tried to keep things going as they had been, did not communicate well, and did not problem solve effectively with her team. As a direct result, several key leaders were contemplating leaving their positions. By contrast, the owner of a different medium-sized organization had worked hard to listen, communicate on a weekly basis, and ground her employees' actions in what could be done. Her employees were incredibly loyal and focused, and the organization was succeeding financially.

Uncertainty is a constant companion in our rapidly changing world and our workplaces, but the amount of uncertainty we face fluctuates. Our leadership responses will do one of two things: they will either contribute to the uncertainty and the resulting stress and anxiety for employees, or help create order, focus, and a path forward. We all take cues about how to behave and even how to feel about things from the people around us, especially those whose influence shapes our lives – our leaders.

SURVEY STATISTICS

We were interested to see what factors were strongly correlated to the statement, "When the world outside of my organization changes, our leaders are quick to adapt." Notably, we found that *adapting to change* and *trust between leaders and staff* are closely connected. 97 percent of those who strongly agreed that there is a high level of trust also indicated that their leaders are quick to adapt to change, versus 18 percent for those who strongly disagreed.

Looking back at the height of the pandemic and to other periods of uncertainty that I have experienced as a leader over the past couple of decades, I can see some valuable lessons that leaders should remember in their efforts to deal with present unknowns. To face these challenges, leaders can anchor their responses in the knowledge that periods of heightened uncertainty will pass with time. When a leader expresses their anxiety about the immediate future in strong ways, followers start to panic, which may lead to self-protective behavior like preparing resumes or, in the case of a pandemic, hoarding toilet paper.

I have also learned that people can experience psychological pain from the stress, anxiety, and fear caused by periods of uncertainty. They may also suffer the very real pain of reduced financial means. Healthy leadership responses acknowledge that we cannot avoid all pain, but we can take steps to reduce the impact of uncertain times and help people through to the other side.

Based on our own experiences of navigating challenging circumstances at ACHIEVE, I have learned that the following strategies help reduce the impact of uncertainty and lead to greater focus and calm action.

Remain Focused on Your Mission and Values

It is easy to get distracted by external concerns and invest too much attention in how to respond to the immediate crisis. Although we need to be prudent and think through our plans for when things are difficult, we also need to keep our organization and staff focused on our reason for existing, our core services, and how we want to behave as we work. If we lose focus on our mission and values, or our reason for existing in the first place, we get lost and anxiety and stress follow.

It's precisely during periods of uncertainty that leaders need to ground their actions and those of the people they lead in meaningful work related to the organization's mission. While external conditions may affect the way an organization can function, in most cases they won't affect whether the organization's mission is still valuable. Leaders should be asking staff to answer the question, "Given the current conditions, how can we work toward our mission?" The way work is done may change, but the mission will not.

Stay Calm

Remember that others look to leaders for guidance, and your emotions and expressions will be felt, scrutinized, and interpreted. As a leader, your voice is amplified by your position of influence and power. When a leader panics, so do their followers. When a leader shouts, employees cower. So, take time to compose yourself each day. If you need to express your anxieties or frustrations, do so quietly with other leaders, then turn your attention back to your mission and values, your work, and your plans.

When a leader expresses their anxiety about the immediate future in strong ways, followers start to panic.

When you present to other staff, customers, clients, or stakeholders, focus on creating calm by being calm. If you remain grounded, it will help others do the same. In order for staff to function at their best, they need you to be an anchor point of calm and rational thought.

Be Realistic in Your Communication

Uncertainty can cause people to exaggerate or minimize risks. Being realistic means taking stock of the assets and strengths you already have as well as your potential vulnerabilities. Given the limitations of your own single perspective, being realistic also means staying attuned to what is happening around you and seeking a variety of perspectives from people both inside and outside of your organization. It means looking for reliable news sources.

As you gather information, plan for both contingency *and* normal operations, always relying on your strengths and assets. Be transparent about risks as you communicate with staff, partners, and clients, but also remind people of the organization's strengths and assets. Work *with* your staff to build a plan based on realistic information. When people have realistic information and a plan based on realism, they can focus on their work and their fears will subside.

Take the Long View

Uncertain times will pass, and every leader's goal should be to create order now and see the organization through to better times. Uncertainty fades as we work together in the now to deal with risks and ambiguity. While uncertain times often bring a measure of pain, they also bring growth when we emerge from them.

Ask yourself what your world looks like on the other side of the uncertainty. Where do you want to be as an organization? Keep your eyes focused on a promising future while you work toward it in the now. As you focus on your mission and the future you envision, you will also create the conditions you need to operate in the present.

Show Compassion

Some people within our organizations are more susceptible to the disturbances created by uncertainty. Their susceptibility comes from having fewer resources, whether they are emotional, physical, or financial. Leaders must stay attuned to those who may be more exposed and do what they can to help mitigate risk for them. For example, during the COVID-19 pandemic, our workplace clearly communicated that staff would be supported to work from home and to stay home if they were sick while receiving pay through our benefits program. Not only did this decrease the risk of someone coming to the office while they were sick and exposing others to the virus, but it also meant that our staff had less anxiety and were able to focus on their work.

When uncertainty is heightened, consider which people are more at risk or perceive themselves to be at risk, and then ask yourself what you can do as a leader to show compassion and to provide resources. As you provide support to individuals at risk, you strengthen their ability to continue working during challenging times. Ultimately this helps you retain your valuable staff and continue the work of your organization through periods of uncertainty.

At ACHIEVE, we have discovered that we can flourish during periods of uncertainty. Although initially we keenly felt the effects of the pandemic, our leadership focused on remaining calm, communicating with realism, taking the long view, and being compassionate. We focused on fulfilling our mission in new and creative ways, and we found a way forward that has been profitable and fulfilling. Uncertainty will pass, and it will come again, so we will take these lessons with us into the future.

REFLECTION QUESTIONS

1. Think back to your own experience with a period of uncertainty such as the COVID-19 pandemic. How did the leaders around you respond? What led you to feel increased anxiety? What helped you feel calm enough to move to action?
2. How does your organization currently deal with uncertainty? What responses have been helpful to staff? What could you be doing more effectively?

PRACTICAL APPLICATION

Ask a trusted colleague to rank you on a scale of 1 to 5 in terms of your ability to remain calm during a crisis. Welcome the feedback and ask what they observed that led them to give you that score. Then consider other ways to reinforce your ability to remain calm.

ADDITIONAL RESOURCE

Our Iceberg Is Melting: Changing and Succeeding Under Any Conditions by John Kotter and Holger Rathgeber (Portfolio, 2016)

53

DON'T STOP LEARNING

BY RANDY GRIESER

While I only cook about once a week, sometimes I like to try making something new beyond my go-to meals of spaghetti and hamburgers. By no means am I a chef, but I do have some cooking instincts. And given that I'm not very patient, I don't have the desire to read long and convoluted recipes, and I definitely don't have the patience to watch a video of someone teaching me how to cook. As a result of my limited culinary knowledge and my lack of desire to learn more before trying a new meal idea, my dishes don't always turn out that great.

I used to approach my development as a leader in the same way I do my cooking. Early on in our organization's existence, I wasn't intentional about developing my leadership skills. I did have some instincts and natural aptitudes that made things easier, but due to the demands of leadership, that wasn't enough, and I would sometimes flounder.

After one too many missteps in my leadership role, I realized that I actually had to work at becoming an effective leader. I needed to become more aware of the areas in which I needed to grow and be more intentional about reading, thinking, and talking about leadership with others. The natural result of this focus on and attention to my development was that I became a better leader.

Like cooking or any other skill, our leadership won't improve until we learn, practice, and give focused attention to our development. And like any skill, it takes more than attending one workshop or reading one book to significantly improve. Leadership development is a life-long journey that never ends. In this last year, I have faced challenges and made mistakes that I haven't made previously, and I'm sure the same will be true for the years ahead. As a result, I have to stay focused on my ongoing development to continue to be an effective leader.

In what follows I highlight six different ways I practice leadership development. You should expect that some will feel more natural and comfortable to you than others, while others may be new to you. While I believe that using multiple methods to learn and grow is more valuable than just focusing on one, when it comes to leadership development the key is to be persistent and consistent with whatever methods you choose.

Training

Hearing from others who have dedicated time and energy to a specific topic is a great way to learn. A good trainer will distill critical information in an understandable and digestible way. There are so many different options to access training including in person or online via on-demand videos or virtually through video conferencing. I personally prefer to access training in person because engaging with a presenter and other workshop participants in live sessions adds valuable depth to the learning experience.

Taking Time to Think

Carving time out of your schedule to think allows us the space to ponder the big-picture questions of leadership. Thinking happens best when we slow down and are not in a rush to move on to something else. It requires us to focus on something for long enough to develop an original and meaningful idea about it. And this can be hard to find without being intentional about setting aside time to just think.

Like cooking or any other skill, our leadership won't improve until we learn, practice, and give focused attention to our development.

Reading

A common theme among effective leaders is that they read. They read the news, their industry's articles, and how-to leadership books. They read to be informed and to improve themselves – not just to increase their knowledge. And of course, most books are available as audio-books, so you can still "read" by listening. One way to enhance reading as a tool for leadership development is to read the same book with your peers and meet to discuss it.

Listening to Podcasts

The number of leadership podcasts is remarkably high and growing. One of the values of podcasts is their ability to generate commentary on current events that leaders face. One reason I like podcasts is that they allow me to multitask. I can listen to a podcast in the car, at the gym, and when walking to work. Interestingly, however, I have found that I do tend to run slower if I listen to a podcast rather than more upbeat music. So, while podcasts are good for my leadership development, they apparently aren't as good for my health.

Informal Conversations with Peers

Having conversations with other leaders is one of the best ways to develop. Most of us are surrounded by other leaders in our work-places, so use these connections and grab a coffee or meet for lunch to talk about the latest leadership book you read, or a problem one of you need help solving. Peers are a great resource for exploring ways of addressing leadership challenges, as well as opportunities.

Formal Conversations with Peers

Intentional, focused conversations with peers are one of my favorite ways to develop as a leader. One of the best approaches is to have a regular (monthly, bimonthly, quarterly) gathering of leadership peers where you consider the following questions:

- What is the biggest relational challenge you are currently dealing with, and what have you done about it thus far?
- What is the biggest operational challenge you are currently dealing with, and what have you done about it thus far?

Each leader should take a turn answering one or both questions. Those listening should then ask clarifying questions and only provide advice once the person has answered their questions and has said what is on their mind. It's important to expect that not every leader will have both a pressing relational and operational challenge to explore.

This is an exercise we do several times a year with our own leadership team. I prefer that, when we come together for this purpose, these two questions are the main part of the agenda. This allows us to deeply consider issues and develop plans for addressing the big challenges some of us are navigating.

SURVEY STATISTICS

When our survey respondents were asked to select their preferred methods of leadership development, they indicated the following preferences:

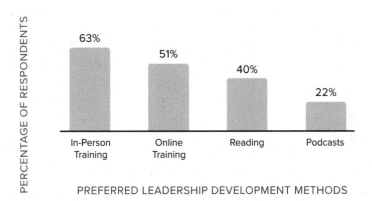

PREFERRED LEADERSHIP DEVELOPMENT METHODS

This same order of preference applies to all age brackets and experience levels; the only exception is that those who had been leading for 20+ years slightly preferred reading over online training.

Older respondents were also a little more likely to pick just one or two methods of development, while younger respondents tended to select a greater variety. Here are the number of selections for preferred development methods by age:

- **Ages 18–39:** average of 2.14 selections per person
- **Ages 40–55:** average of 1.87 selections per person
- **Ages 56+:** average of 1.59 selections per person

In-person training is the most popular method for leaders of any age, but younger leaders tend to use a greater variety of approaches for leadership development. This could indicate that, as leaders age, they are less open to new methods of learning. Or perhaps it indicates that, over time, they discover the development methods that work best for them and do not feel the need to use other methods.

Find more statistics about reading, podcasts, and online or in-person training habits of leaders on pages 277–281 in the Survey Analysis section.

Leadership development is a journey that takes time and requires work. We don't "get there" – we don't arrive at a place when we are "finished" developing as a leader. It takes time and effort, but it does occur more quickly and easily when you are focused and have a plan for your own development.

REFLECTION QUESTIONS

1. What do you currently do to develop as a leader? How much time do you spend focusing on leadership development? Do you need to dedicate more time and energy to your development?
2. What is your future leadership development plan? How much time and in what different ways will you commit to developing as a leader?

PRACTICAL APPLICATION

In the next two months, gather your leadership team for the sole purpose of considering the two questions noted in the "Formal Conversations with Peers" section of this insight.

ADDITIONAL RESOURCES

The Leadership Challenge: How to Make Extraordinary Things Happen in Organizations by James Kouzes and Barry Posner (Wiley, 2017)

TED Talk: "What It Takes to Be a Great Leader" by Roselinde Torres

CONCLUSION

You've invested a lot of time into reading this book, so now what? We encourage you to develop a plan. If you spent weeks or months reading this book, we hope you've already been trying out some of the practical application ideas we've shared. But if not, now is the time to take the next step and implement any changes or strategies you have identified through your reading.

Grab a notepad and pen or open up a blank document on your computer to record a plan. In the months ahead, refer to this plan to see if you've implemented your ideas and reflect on how they have worked. If you've stalled in your application of an idea, recommit to it or reconsider and update it.

We want to inspire leaders to action through this book and hope that you continue your leadership development now that you're finished reading. Treat your workplace like a garden and create conditions in which people can thrive. Continue to become a more skillful gardener by seeking out new ways to develop as a leader, and don't blame yourself or others when something doesn't work, or someone doesn't thrive. Instead, seek to understand, to develop yourself and others, and to change the growing conditions. And remember, leadership development is an ongoing journey – there is *always* more to learn.

SURVEY ANALYSIS

Throughout this book, we have referenced statistics from our Leadership Development Survey. We collected responses from 1,188 people who identify as leaders from organizations of diverse sizes and in a variety of industries. Participants responded to 36 questions divided into three types: multiple choice, Likert-type scale, and long answer.

Here is a sample of the findings we explore in more detail in this section:

- A workplace culture is more likely to be healthy when staff report that their leaders care about them as people.
- The more senior you are as a leader, the more likely you are to be prioritized for leadership development opportunities.
- Leaders list *time* as a more common barrier to their development than *money*.
- Among online training, books, and podcasts, leaders still choose in-person training as their preferred method of development.

Responses were collected by posting the survey on our website, sharing it on our social media feeds, and emailing current clients and contacts to see if they would like to participate. As this was not a randomized sampling method, we cannot be certain that our results accurately reflect the opinions of the general population. While we cannot determine the statistical significance of our survey results for the general population, we believe the results of this survey are *practically and operationally significant*. This means that our survey results provide insights into the ways various factors interact in developing great leaders and healthy workplaces.

For the Likert scale questions, participants were asked to rate 20 statements on a five-point scale, choosing from Strongly Disagree, Disagree, Neutral, Agree, and Strongly Agree. For the purposes of this analysis, all answers of Strongly Agree and Agree are considered to be in agreement with the statement in question, while Disagree and Strongly Disagree are considered to be in disagreement. Any numbers in this report that do not add up to 100 percent are due to rounding to the nearest whole number.

We also analyzed our data to find any significant correlations. Correlation measures the strength of the relationship between variables, showing us how often people give similar answers to two different questions. This relationship is expressed with the coefficient "r." Coefficient values range from -1 (strong negative relationship) to 1 (strong positive relationship). When looking at positive relationships, coefficients of 0 to 0.19 are considered to have no significant relationship, 0.2 to 0.39 are considered weak, 0.4 to 0.59 are considered moderate, and 0.6 to 1 are considered strong. A strong correlation does not indicate that there is a causal relationship between the variables, but it does, at least, suggest that the two go hand in hand.

The following analysis includes statistics and relationships that we found notable in the areas of workplace culture, leadership qualities, and leadership development.

My organization has a healthy workplace culture.

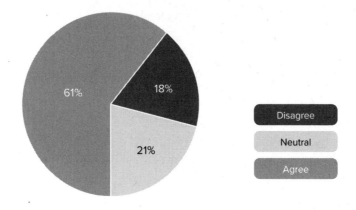

Over half of our respondents reported that their organization has a healthy workplace culture. While 61 percent agreed, 21 percent were neutral, and 18 percent disagreed. The strongest correlated statement with "My organization has a healthy workplace culture" was, "There is a high level of trust between staff and leaders in my organization" (r=0.71). The second strongest correlated statement was, "Leaders in my organization demonstrate care for their staff" (r=0.63).

There were some significant differences between those who reported that they have a healthy workplace culture and those who said their workplace culture is unhealthy when correlated with the statements in the left-hand column below.

SURVEY STATEMENT	Percentage of those who agreed with the survey statement *and* said their workplace has a *healthy* culture	Percentage of those who agreed with the survey statement *and* said their workplace has an *unhealthy* culture	Correlation Value
There is a high level of trust between staff and leaders in my organization.	68%	4%	r=0.71 (strong)
Leaders in my organization demonstrate care for their staff.	87%	24%	r=0.63 (strong)
My organization values leadership development.	86%	38%	r=0.56 (moderate)
When the world outside of my organization changes, our leaders are quick to adapt.	79%	28%	r=0.55 (moderate)
My organization emphasizes people skills as part of leadership development.	87%	35%	r=0.53 (moderate)
Leaders in my organization develop as a result of learning from each other.	84%	43%	r=0.48 (moderate)

Respondents in both healthy and unhealthy workplaces agreed that leaders play a key role in a workplace's health. Of those who indicated they work in a healthy workplace, 99 percent agreed with the statement, "The role of a leader is critical to creating healthy workplace cultures," along with 94 percent of respondents who indicated they work in an unhealthy workplace.

Smaller organizations tended to have healthier workplace cultures than larger ones. Here is the percentage of respondents who reported that they have a healthy workplace culture, by organization size:

- **69%** from organizations with 1–15 employees
- **62%** from organizations with 16–150 employees
- **55%** from organizations with 151+ employees

The healthcare and government sectors reported the lowest rates of healthy workplace culture. This is the percentage of leaders from each sector who reported having a healthy workplace culture:

- **70%** from the business sector
- **65%** from the social services sector
- **64%** from the education sector
- **53%** from the government sector
- **48%** from the healthcare sector

There is a high level of trust between staff and leaders in my organization.

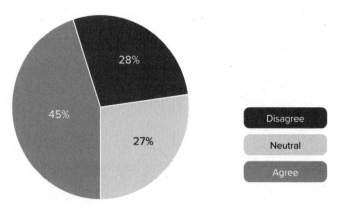

Overall, only 45 percent of respondents agreed with the statement, "There is a high level of trust between staff and leaders in my organization." The strongest correlated statement was "My organization has a healthy workplace culture" (r=0.71). Of respondents who reported high levels of trust between staff and leaders, 91 percent also reported having a healthy workplace culture as opposed to 17 percent of those who reported low levels of trust.

We can clearly see that leaders influence workplace culture. The strongest indicator of a healthy workplace culture across all sectors is whether there is trust between leaders and staff, followed closely by whether leaders demonstrate care for their staff, as seen in the chart below.

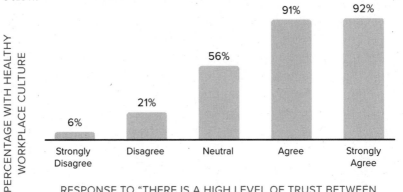

RESPONSE TO "THERE IS A HIGH LEVEL OF TRUST BETWEEN STAFF AND LEADERS IN MY ORGANIZATION"

There tended to be higher levels of trust between leaders and staff in smaller organizations than in larger ones, as demonstrated in the chart below.

SIZE OF ORGANIZATION

While the majority of leaders did not report high levels of trust between leaders and staff in their workplace, our research clearly indicates that levels of trust are closely tied to the health of a workplace culture. The relationship between an organization's size and levels of trust shows that staff are more likely to trust their leaders in smaller organizations.

Leaders in my organization demonstrate care for their staff.

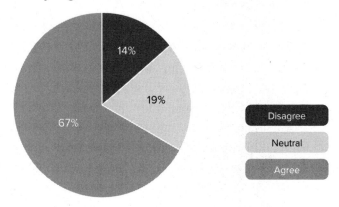

The strongest correlated statement with "Leaders in my organization demonstrate care for their staff" was "There is a high level of trust between staff and leaders in my organization" (r=0.70). Of the respondents who reported that leaders at their organization care for their staff, 63 percent also reported high levels of trust between leaders and staff, as opposed to 4 percent from organizations where leaders do not demonstrate care for their staff, as illustrated in the chart below.

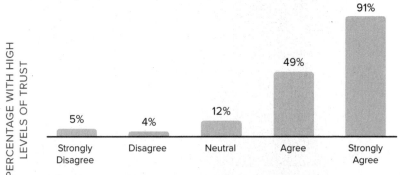

The second strongest correlated statement to "Leaders in my organization demonstrate care for their staff" was "My organization has a healthy workplace culture." Of those who agreed with the statement, "Leaders in my organization demonstrate care for their staff," 73 percent also reported that their organization has a healthy workplace culture, as opposed to 13 percent of those who disagreed with the statement.

There is also a moderate correlation between the statements "Leaders in my organization demonstrate care for their staff" and "My organization emphasizes people skills as part of leadership development" (r=0.54). Of the respondents from organizations that emphasize people skills, 78 percent reported that leaders in their organizations demonstrate care for staff, as opposed to 25 percent of respondents from organizations where people skills are not emphasized.

In summary, there is a strong correlation between leaders who care for their staff and leaders who are trusted by their staff. Notably, almost no respondents reported high levels of trust in organizations where leaders do not demonstrate care. As stated earlier, care shown to staff by leaders is closely related to healthier workplace cultures.

I am confident in my leadership abilities at work.

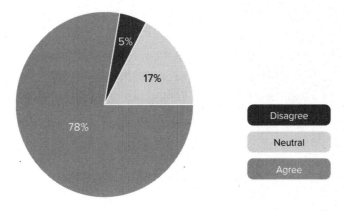

The strongest correlated statement with "I am confident in my leadership abilities at work" was "I have a clear philosophy of leadership" (r=0.56). Of those who reported they have a clear philosophy of leadership, 90 percent feel confident in their leadership abilities, as opposed to 32 percent of those who do not have a clear leadership philosophy. This is illustrated in the chart below.

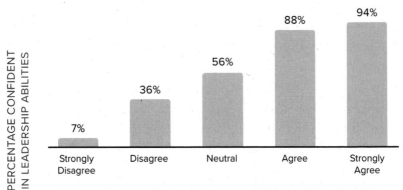

RESPONSE TO "I HAVE A CLEAR PHILOSOPHY OF LEADERSHIP"

The second strongest correlated statement was "I make time for my own development as a leader each year" (r=0.48). Of respondents who make time for their own development, 83 percent reported having confidence in their leadership abilities, as opposed to 32 percent of those who do not make time for leadership development.

It should be no surprise that those who take the time for their own leadership development are more confident in their abilities and have a clear philosophy of leadership. Being intentional about learning and skill development will inevitably increase a leader's confidence and competence.

My organization's leaders have a congruent philosophy of leadership.

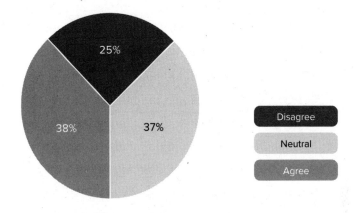

While it is fairly common for leaders to have their own clear philosophy of leadership, it is much less likely that their personal philosophy lines up with the philosophies of other leaders at their organization. Whereas 71 percent of respondents agreed with the statement, "I have a clear philosophy of leadership," only 38 percent of all respondents agreed with the statement, "My organization's leaders have a congruent philosophy of leadership."

The strongest correlated statement with "My organization's leaders have a congruent philosophy of leadership" was "There is a high level of trust between staff and leaders in my organization" (r=0.62). Of respondents who felt their organization has a congruent leadership philosophy, 75 percent also reported high levels of trust between leadership and staff, as opposed to 10 percent of respondents who said there is not a congruent leadership philosophy. As you can see in the chart below, it seems congruent leadership and trust are closely connected.

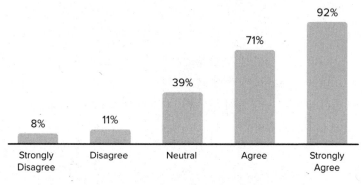

RESPONSE TO "MY ORGANIZATION'S LEADERS HAVE
A CONGRUENT PHILOSOPHY OF LEADERSHIP"

Organizations in the social services sector tended to have higher rates of a congruent leadership philosophy than other industries, as shown in the chart below.

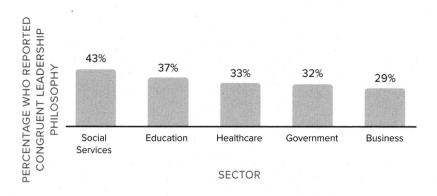

SECTOR

It stands to reason that a shared philosophy of leadership is closely tied to the level of trust between leaders and staff. When leaders have a consistent leadership philosophy, staff don't have to question how leaders will react in a given situation – they can trust that they'll be treated fairly and consistently, no matter who they're dealing with. Notably, very few respondents reported high levels of trust when their organization's leaders do not have a congruent leadership philosophy.

My organization provides opportunities for me to develop as a leader.

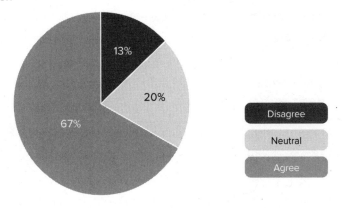

Sixty-seven percent of all respondents reported that their organization provides opportunities for them to develop as a leader, and 64 percent reported that their organization pays for their leadership development.

Below is the percentage of respondents who reported that their organization pays for leadership development, organized by experience level.

Although there may be other factors at play, these findings illustrate how organizations are more likely to pay for development opportunities as the experience level of the leader goes up.

What makes a great leader?

When survey respondents were asked to describe the characteristics of a great leader, many similar themes came up in their long-answer question responses. The most frequently reported characteristic was *listener*, followed by *communicator, empathetic*, and *open*.

The following list contains the top 15 ways respondents described a great leader and the number of times they occurred in the responses:

	WORD/WORDS	NUMBER OF USES
1	Listen, listener, listening, listens	299
2	Communicate, communicates, communicator, communication	240
3	Empathetic, empathic, empathy	167
4	Open, openness	162
5	Learn, learning, learner	154
6	Integrity	142
7	Honest, honesty	130
8	Support, supportive	127
9	Trust, trusting, trustworthy, trusts	125
10	Vision, visionary	110
11	Care, cares, caring	102
12	Knowledge, knows, knowledgeable	100
13	Respect, respectful, respects, respectfully	97
14	Compassion, compassionate	96
15	Encourage, encouraging	89

The following visualization shows the relative frequency with which the various words were used in descriptions of great leadership by size of word:

These word choices suggest that the most important qualities that make a leader great include being a good listener and communicator who approaches staff with empathy and openness.

What are the barriers to leadership development?

Participants were given the long-answer question, "When it comes to engaging in regular leadership development opportunities, what obstacles do you face?" By far the most frequently noted obstacle was *time*, which was used a total of 699 times. The second most frequently noted obstacle was *finances*.

The following is a list of the top 15 obstacles to leadership development as noted by respondents:

	WORD/WORDS	NUMBER OF USES
1	Time, busy	728
2	Budget, cost, expensive, finances, funding, money	301
3	Opportunities, opportunity	182
4	Organization, company, agency	84
5	Support	75
6	Finding	60
7	Pandemic, COVID*	56
8	Schedule, scheduling	38
9	Role, roles	38
10	Priorities, priority	36
11	Location, local	29
12	Family	26
13	Availability	26
14	Workload	24
15	Responsibilities	18

* This survey was conducted during the COVID-19 pandemic.

The following visualization shows the relative strength of the top barriers to leadership development by size of word:

The most significant barrier to personal development for most leaders is a lack of time. Financial resources, the support of their organization, and available opportunities were secondary barriers, but were listed less than half as often.

What are the preferred leadership development methods?
When asked to select all their preferred methods of leadership development, respondents indicated a preference for in-person training, as seen below.

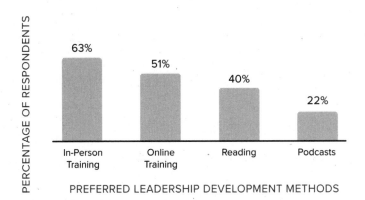

This same order of preference applies to all age brackets and experience levels; the only exception is that those who had been leading for 20+ years slightly preferred reading over online training.

Older respondents were also more likely to pick just one or two methods of development, while younger respondents tended to select a greater variety. In-person training is the most popular method for leaders of any age, but younger leaders tend to use a greater variety of approaches for leadership development. This could indicate that, as leaders age, they are less open to new methods of learning. Or perhaps it indicates that, over time, they discover the development methods that work best for them and do not feel the need to use other methods.

Here are the number of selections for preferred development methods by age:

- **Ages 18–39:** average of 2.14 selections per person
- **Ages 40–55:** average of 1.87 selections per person
- **Ages 56+:** average of 1.59 selections per person

Reading

When asked the average number of books per year they read for leadership development, most respondents indicated that they read one or two books per year, as illustrated in the chart below.

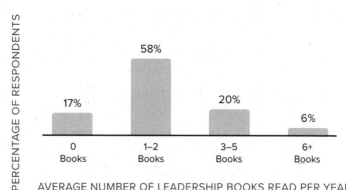

In general, older leaders read more books and younger leaders read less. Only 19 percent of leaders between the ages of 18 and 39 reported reading an average of three or more leadership books per year, as opposed to 26 percent of leaders who are 40 and older.

When asked the number of books they read per year, most new leaders and experienced leaders indicated that they read one or two books per year, as seen in the chart below.

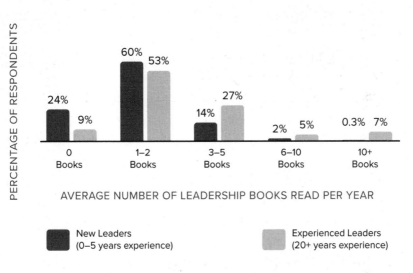

AVERAGE NUMBER OF LEADERSHIP BOOKS READ PER YEAR

New Leaders (0–5 years experience)

Experienced Leaders (20+ years experience)

In total, 16 percent of respondents had participated in a leadership development book study. Those in the public sector (19 percent) and the not-for-profit sector (13 percent) reported higher participation in a leadership book club or study, as opposed to 6 percent of those in the private sector.

Leaders in the business sector read more books per year on average than leaders in other sectors. On average, 25 percent of all leaders reported reading three or more leadership books per year, compared to 41 percent of those in the business sector.

While the majority of leaders read one or two leadership books per year, leadership book studies are rarely used as a form of leadership development. More experienced leaders and leaders from the business sector tend to read a greater number of leadership books per year.

Podcasts

When asked the average number of hours per week they spend listening to podcasts for leadership development, just under half of all leaders spend some time listening to leadership podcasts in an average week, as seen in the chart below.

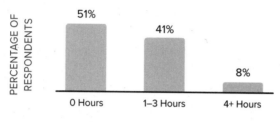

AVERAGE HOURS PER WEEK SPENT
LISTENING TO LEADERSHIP PODCASTS

In-Person and Online Training

When asked the average number of in-person leadership training events they attend per year, a strong majority of respondents reported that they participate in at least one in-person training in an average year, as seen in the chart below.

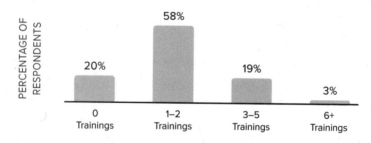

AVERAGE NUMBER OF IN-PERSON
LEADERSHIP TRAININGS ATTENDED PER YEAR

Older leaders tend to do slightly more in-person training than younger leaders, as illustrated in the chart below.

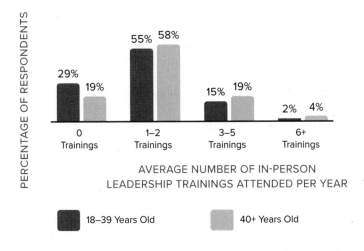

Younger respondents were somewhat more likely than older participants to select online training as one of their preferred methods of development. Of respondents ages 18–39, 60 percent indicated online training as one of their preferred methods of development, as opposed to 49 percent of respondents ages 40 and over.

In-person training is the most popular method of personal leadership development for all ages and experience levels. On average, older leaders attend more in-person workshops and read more books, while younger leaders typically use more online training and a greater variety of methods for their personal development.

The intention of our survey was to explore practices related to effective leadership and leadership development and what our findings might teach us about creating and maintaining healthy workplaces. We are deeply grateful to all those who participated in providing this data.

REFERENCES

Introduction *Page IX*

1. Thich Nhat Hanh, *Peace Is Every Step: The Path of Mindfulness in Everyday Life* (New York: Bantam Books, 1992).

Don't Blame the Lettuce *Page 1*

1. Thich Nhat Hanh, *Peace Is Every Step: The Path of Mindfulness in Everyday Life* (New York: Bantam Books, 1992).

Why Vulnerability Makes a Better Leader *Page 35*

1. Brené Brown, *Daring Greatly: How the Courage to Be Vulnerable Transforms the Way We Live, Love, Parent, and Lead* (New York: Gotham Books, 2012), 2.

Let It Go *Page 39*

1. Randy Grieser, *The Ordinary Leader: 10 Key Insights for Building and Leading a Thriving Organization* (Winnipeg: ACHIEVE Publishing, 2017), 150.

Support Mental Health at Work *Page 79*

1. Carley Sime, "The Cost Of Ignoring Mental Health In The Workplace," *Forbes*, April 17, 2019, https://www.forbes.com/sites/carleysime/2019/04/17/the-cost-of-ignoring-mental-health-in-the-workplace/#d94d2043726a.

2. Hannah Ritchie, "Global Mental Health: Five Key Insights Which Emerge from the Data," *Our World in Data*. Global Change Data Lab, May 16, 2018, https://ourworldindata.org/global-mental-health.

What My Concussion Taught Me about Resilience *Page 93*

1. "Resilience," *Merriam-Webster*, accessed December 9, 2020, https://www.merriam-webster.com/dictionary/resilience.

The Secret to Building Trust *Page 98*

1. Randy Grieser, Eric Stutzman, Wendy Loewen, and Michael Labun, *The Culture Question: How to Create a Workplace Where People Like to Work* (Winnipeg: ACHIEVE Publishing, 2019), 191.

Move Beyond Gender Equality *Page 117*

1. "The Global Gender Gap Report 2018," *World Economic Forum*, 2018, https://www.weforum.org/reports/the-global-gender-gap-report-2018.
2. "Women in Leadership Survey Analysis," *ACHIEVE Centre for Leadership*, 2020, https://ca.achievecentre.com/wp-content/uploads/2020/09/ACHIEVE-Women-in-Leadership-Survey-Analysis1.pdf.
3. Stefanie K. Johnson, David R. Hekman, and Elsa T. Chan, "If There's Only One Woman in Your Candidate Pool, There's Statistically No Chance She'll Be Hired," *Harvard Business Review*, April 26, 2016, https://hbr.org/2016/04/if-theres-only-one-woman-in-your-candidate-pool-theres-statistically-no-chance-shell-be-hired.
4. Stefanie K. Johnson, David R. Hekman, and Elsa T. Chan, "If There's Only One Woman in Your Candidate Pool, There's Statistically No Chance She'll Be Hired," *Harvard Business Review*, April 26, 2016, https://hbr.org/2016/04/if-theres-only-one-woman-in-your-candidate-pool-theres-statistically-no-chance-shell-be-hired.
5. "Women in Leadership Survey Analysis," *ACHIEVE Centre for Leadership*, 2020, https://ca.achievecentre.com/wp-content/uploads/2020/09/ACHIEVE-Women-in-Leadership-Survey-Analysis1.pdf.

Lead with a Sense of Urgency *Page 122*

1. John P. Kotter, *A Sense of Urgency* (Boston: Harvard Business Review Press, 2008), 12.

Are You Controlling or Connecting? *Page 127*

1. Clifford Nass and Corina Yen, *The Man Who Lied to His Laptop: What We Can Learn About Ourselves from Our Machines* (London: Current, 2012).

Always Tell the Truth *Page 133*

1. Russell Hotten, "Volkswagen: The Scandal Explained," *BBC News*, December 10, 2015, https://www.bbc.com/news/business-34324772.

2. Ann Skeet, "The Volkswagen Brand Crisis," *Markkula Center for Applied Ethics*, December 30, 2015, https://www.scu.edu/ethics/leadership-ethics-blog/the-volkswagen-brand-crisis/.

3. Russell Hotten, "Volkswagen: The Scandal Explained," *BBC News*, December 10, 2015, https://www.bbc.com/news/business-34324772.

4. Victor Lipman, "The Most Important Leadership Attribute? New Study Has Clear Answer," *Forbes*, October 25, 2016, https://www.forbes.com/sites/victorlipman/2016/10/25/the-most-important-leadership-attribute-new-study-has-clear-answer/?sh=296de9324df2.

5. Zorana Ivcevic, Jochen I. Menges, and Anna Miller, "How Common Is Unethical Behavior in U.S. Organizations?" *Harvard Business Review*, March 20, 2020, https://hbr.org/2020/03/how-common-is-unethical-behavior-in-u-s-organizations.

What Are Your Workplace Rituals? *Page 183*

1. Mollie West and Kate McCoubrey Judson, "Want to Strengthen Workplace Culture? Design a Ritual," *HuffPost Business*, August 26, 2016, https://www.huffpost.com/entry/want-to-strengthen-workpl_b_11730914?guccounter=1.

Creating a Psychologically Safe Workplace *Page 187*

1. Charles Duhigg, "What Google Learned From Its Quest to Build the Perfect Team," *The New York Times Magazine*, February 25, 2016, https://www.nytimes.com/2016/02/28/magazine/what-google-learned-from-its-quest-to-build-the-perfect-team.html?smid=pl-share.

2. Amy C. Edmondson, "Building a Psychologically Safe Workplace," TED Talk, May 5, 2014, 11:26, https://www.youtube.com/watch?v=LhoLuui9gX8.

What I Learned about Purpose from Patagonia *Page 192*

1. Simon Sinek, *Start with Why: How Great Leaders Inspire Everyone to Take Action* (New York: Portfolio, 2009), 39.

What Will Happen When You're Not There? *Page 220*

1. Michael T. Deane, "Top 6 Reasons New Businesses Fail," *Investopedia*, August 28, 2020, https://www.investopedia.com/financial-edge/1010/top-6-reasons-new-businesses-fail.aspx.

Taking the Mystery Out of Innovation *Page 225*

1. Randy Grieser, *The Ordinary Leader: 10 Key Insights for Building and Leading a Thriving Organization* (Winnipeg: ACHIEVE Publishing, 2017), 126.

Is It Time to Terminate Performance Reviews? *Page 230*

1. Jena McGregor, "Study Finds That Basically Every Single Person Hates Performance Reviews," *The Washington Post*, January 27, 2014, https://www.washingtonpost.com/news/on-leadership/wp/2014/01/27/study-finds-that-basically-every-single-person-hates-performance-reviews/.

Building a Great Team *Page 240*

1. Jim Collins, *Good to Great: Why Some Companies Make the Leap... and Others Don't* (New York: Harper Business, 2001), 41.

Why Your Vibe Matters *Page 245*

1. Natalie Mendes and Prashant Kukde, "How Do Emotions Affect Productivity? [New Research]," *Atlassian*, November 29, 2017, https://www.atlassian.com/blog/software-teams/new-research-emotional-intelligence-in-the-workplace.

ACKNOWLEDGMENTS

We are thankful for the many people who have assisted in bringing this book to completion. This project has been the work of many hands.

In particular, we want to thank Tyler Voth, ACHIEVE's internal editor, who read and provided feedback on the manuscript at every step along the way. In addition, we want to acknowledge the role of Erin Sawatzky and Micah Zerbe, who analyzed our survey responses and wrote the first draft of the book's Survey Analysis section.

Thank you to Janelle Jackiw, Heidi Grieser, and Mark Schinkel, who read and provided feedback on the manuscript. We are grateful for the skill and watchful eye of our editor Jessica Antony, and for our proofreader Brenda Boughton. A big thank you to Lisa Friesen – her creativity resulted in a fabulous book cover and interior design.

We want to express our appreciation to the 1,284 people who participated in the survey we conducted for this book. Your responses provided rich material, and we thank you for sharing your insights and opinions.

Finally, we are eternally grateful to our families, who supported us in many different ways as we wrote this book. Thank you for your thoughtfulness and patience. We love you.

ADDITIONAL RESOURCES

Blogs

Eric, Wendy, and Randy regularly write blog posts about leadership and workplace culture. You can find Eric and Wendy's posts in the Free Resources section of ACHIEVE's website at www.achievecentre.com. Randy's blog can be found at www.theordinaryleader.com.

ACHIEVE Workplace Culture Podcast

To listen to Eric, Wendy, and Randy's monthly podcast, subscribe to our newsletter or connect with us wherever you get your podcasts to listen to new episodes.

Free Workplace Cultural Health Assessment Tool

Are you looking for a more accurate picture of your organization's health? ACHIEVE has a free Workplace Cultural Health Assessment available on our website in the Free Resources section. This assessment normally takes between two and five minutes to complete. You will be provided with an eight-page report that will help you evaluate, understand, and discuss your organization's culture.

Training

ACHIEVE Centre for Leadership has over 40 different workshop topics in the areas of leadership development, workplace culture, and conflict resolution. We have a workshop based on this book: *Leadership Insights – Ideas to Take You Further*. All our workshops are designed to help organizations become places where people like to work. View trainings online, attend open-enrollment public workshops in a city near you, or, if you have a group of people to train, one of our facilitators can deliver a workshop at your location.

Keynote Speaking

For your next conference, convention, or meeting, consider having Eric, Wendy, or Randy be your speaker. They provide engaging, inspirational, and humorous 30- to 90-minute presentations on topics related to leadership, workplace culture, conflict, and engagement.

For more information:

ACHIEVE
CENTRE FOR LEADERSHIP

www.achievecentre.com
info@achievecentre.com
877-270-9776

ABOUT THE AUTHORS AND ACHIEVE CENTRE FOR LEADERSHIP

Eric Stutzman

Eric is the Chief Executive Officer of ACHIEVE Centre for Leadership and co-author of *The Culture Question*. He is a Chartered Mediator with diverse experience working in the field of conflict resolution. Eric has a particular interest and skill set in helping groups experiencing conflict bring about stability and resolution. He is an insightful leader who believes that building authentic relationships is the best way to lead people effectively. In his spare time, Eric likes to camp, challenge himself on a mountain bike, and listen to his children play folk music.

Wendy Loewen

Wendy is the Managing Director of ACHIEVE Centre for Leadership and co-author of *The Culture Question*. She has a master's degree in Conflict Analysis and Management, and bachelor's degrees in both Psychology and Education. Early in Wendy's career, she was a teacher and director of a health and social service program in a northern Inuit community. She is a thoughtful and empowering leader who believes in the value of listening to people. In her spare time, Wendy likes to read, go for walks on her family farm with a coffee in hand, and host meals with friends.

Eric, Randy, and Wendy

Randy Grieser

Randy is the founder and Chief Vision Officer of ACHIEVE Centre for Leadership, author of *The Ordinary Leader*, and co-author of *The Culture Question* and *A Little Book About Trauma-Informed Workplaces*. Randy has a Master of Social Work degree and, earlier in his career, worked in the field of mental health. He is an intuitive and visionary leader who, together with a team of staff and trainers, has positioned ACHIEVE to be one of the premier providers of professional development training. In his spare time, he likes to travel, go hiking, and eat good cheese.

ACHIEVE Centre for Leadership

We believe that everyone should be able to like where they work. ACHIEVE provides training (in-person and online), consulting, books, and free resources in the areas of leadership, workplace culture, and conflict resolution. Be sure to check out the Free Resources section of our website.